What others have to say about this author and his work

Transforming Trauma Together is not a textbook, it is a workbook. Neil Hockey's autobiographical book invites us to join him on the journey of doing the hard work - indeed the heart work - of transformation. It is written in simple language, but it is not simplistic. It calls us to engage in a complex, multifaceted series of actions and reflections needed to change ourselves and our societies.

Dave Andrews
a Better World

Transforming Trauma [...] act handbook on spiritual and soc[...] ritical space, working at the interf[...] and historical trauma when seeking to bring about lasting change. It demonstrates great clarity and is immensely practical.

Neil's extensive experience of working in community and alongside First Nations Peoples of Queensland, Australia is well complemented in this short work by his academic learning which, although worn lightly, provides a unique perspective on many of today's most critical challenges. In *Transforming Trauma Together* philosophy and the social sciences are brought into dialogue with truth and matters of transforming faith, trust, love, and integrity. Each of the series of brief chapters is followed by suggestions for action. The book is supplemented by a helpful list of further reading.

Transforming Trauma Together needs to be kept close at hand by every person working in situations of social harm, armed conflict or violence.

Ivan Hutnik
Co-founder of Restoring Relations and member of International Conciliation Team, Quaker Peace & Social Witness, Britain Yearly Meeting

In this book Neil often describes and encapsulates concisely the essence of a general or specific trauma within a few sentences, but to me, they can lead to cliffhangers because just as it grabbed my attention, it stopped! Sometimes I had to pay attention to every sentence, using a lot of energy just to read through a couple of pages because each paragraph is so packed. The suggestions for action are very good, provided readers build up their background knowledge.

Chong Mei Lin
Elijah House, Malaysia

Organisations and interventions today need to be innovative for the future. Neil's strong listening and observational skills enable him to work alongside leaders and develop appropriate responses. He can assist your group in navigating through circumstances where you might struggle with barriers to "sustainability and survival".

Mathew Titus
Managing Partner / Market and EcoSystem Advisory.
Former Member, Prime Minister's Council on Micro, Small and Medium Enterprises 2010 – 2014

Vedoostham was an annual Christian Bhakti festival held at the Sattal Christian Ashram in Uttarakhand, India, since 2009. Each speaker needs to be knowledgeable in addressing challenging themes in contemporary contexts. They must also be able to relate well to a very diverse audience in terms of age, gender, cultural background and at times even faiths. Neil challenged his audiences there to join him in exploring ideas and to strive for a deeper understanding by relating his personal journey in faith and social justice through health, healing, education and community work.

Anuvinda Varkey
New Delhi, Former Executive Director of the Christian Coalition for Health, India
Former General Secretary of the YWCA of Delhi

Neil I often look back to the years you spent with us in Ooty. I was struck by your deep commitment to excellence and industry and was regularly provoked and challenged by you to think out of the box in Christian thought and life.

Thomas George
Deputy Principal (retired), Hebron School, Udhagamandalum (Ooty), Nilgiri Hills, South India

---

Neil Hockey was my PhD student. His intellect is anchored in a spirituality deeply impressive in its willingness to acknowledge others' spirituality. He was one of the first thinkers to embrace the famous "spiritual turn" in the Critical Realist movement, led by the late Roy Bhaskar. Neil confronted without fear the deep prejudice in the academy against spirituality. He was also able to establish not only the desirability but also the necessity of approaching First Nations Peoples through recognising the significance to them of their spirituality. Neil will challenge any audience, but that challenge will always be underpinned by a non-judgemental respect for other people.

Gary MacLennan, PhD
Research Officer
Department of Seniors, Disability Services and Aboriginal and Torres Strait Islander Partnerships
Queensland Government

I observed Neil Hockey's speaking and writing in several international conferences over more than a decade. His PhD thesis had a primary focus on Indigenous Peoples or First Nations contexts, both in Australia and globally. It helps to create conditions for effective agency in such contexts while underlabouring for decolonisation. Although he critiques the meta-theoretical framework of relevant academic philosophical and anthropological literature, he develops his argument via a critical engagement with a selection of First Nation thinkers.

Mervyn Hartwig, PhD
University Lecturer (retired), founding editor of *Journal of Critical Realism*, and editor and principal author of *Dictionary of Critical Realism*

Neil Hockey is working in a government funded community project amongst Indigenous family groups. His participatory research was partly designed to show how such projects could be improved. The aim was to make the collaborative work more liberatory for all involved, whether Indigenous or not. Listening to Neil speak and examining his excellent research over five years, I commend his superb account of the methodology for any collaborative research in his field, whether it be geared to emancipating the coloniser or the colonised.

28 May 2007.

Roy Bhaskar, PhD (1944-2014)
World Scholar and Director of the International Centre of Critical Realism,
University of London Institute of Education

TRANSFORMING TRAUMA TOGETHER

Think, Live, and Speak Truth with Integrity

Global Publishing Group
Australia • New Zealand • Singapore • America • London

TRANSFORMING TRAUMA TOGETHER

Think, Live, and Speak Truth with Integrity

Neil Hockey

DISCLAIMER

All the information, techniques, skills and concepts contained within this publication are of the nature of general comment only and are not in any way recommended as individual advice. The intent is to offer a variety of information to provide a wider range of choices now and in the future, recognising that we all have widely diverse circumstances and viewpoints. Should any reader choose to make use of the information contained herein, this is their decision, and the contributors (and their companies), authors and publishers do not assume any responsibilities whatsoever under any condition or circumstances. It is recommended that the reader obtain their own independent advice.

First Edition 2024

Copyright © 2024 Neil Hockey

All rights are reserved. The material contained within this book is protected by copyright law, no part may be copied, reproduced, presented, stored, communicated or transmitted in any form by any means without prior written permission.

National Library of Australia
Cataloguing-in-Publication entry:

Transforming Trauma Together: Think, Live, and Speak Truth with Integrity - Neil Hockey

1st ed.
ISBN: 978-1-925370-86-7 (pbk.)

 A catalogue record for this book is available from the National Library of Australia

Published by Global Publishing Group
PO Box 258, Banyo, QLD 4014 Australia
Email admin@globalpublishinggroup.com.au

For further information about orders:
Phone: +61 7 3267 0747

Dedicated to
all vulnerable children suffering consequences
not of their own making,
that they might flourish
through our relentless commitments
to being transformed.

ACKNOWLEDGEMENTS

In 2020 the inspirational Jeff Goins helped galvanise me into reviving consistent writing habits. Then Grant Baldwin and his exceptional team at The Speaker Lab helped me build the bigger picture. But it was through Nik Cree at SmashGo that I was introduced to Andrew Carter and Jenny Moutou with their consistently invaluable challenges, direction and guidance at Global Publishing Group. Without GPG I would still be wading through endless pages of notes. My heartfelt thanks to you all!

The seeds for transforming trauma together were sown in my experiences of belonging in many communities. You have all helped cultivate both my growth and the writing of this book. Thank you:

- my Hockey and Spall extended families – lifelong sharing stories and histories
- a wide network of families gathering regularly around Wavell Heights
- Virginia and Banyo Schools – so grateful we still meet up after 50-60 years
- student movements and open homes around St Lucia
- semi-rural life in Central Queensland
- Aashiana, Sahara, and related communities in North India
- Hebron School, Udhagamandalam, South India
- the extended Lim families in Malaysia and the UK
- Jubilee Fellowship as a pastoral community in Brisbane
- Goori (Indigenous) families across Logan-Beaudesert.

Among mentors, other close friends and their families who've walked with me over decades, being both incredibly hospitable and speaking the truth in love, I thank you first Charles Ringma for your generous foreword.

Second, Dave Andrews, Ivan Hutnik, Mathew Titus, Anuvinda Varkey, Chong Mei Lin, Tom George, Gary McLennan, Mervyn Hartwig, Roy Bhaskar and Tanya Strydom all very kindly wrote feedback on either this book or my work and writing in other spheres.

I thank Kellie Adams, Justin Hockey, Serena Hockey and Chandrakant Shourie for prompting key revisions of the manuscript. Overall, I've been encouraged in my writing by a widening circle of relatives and friends, including several in the Mueller communities where I now live and work. At the centre of this circle is Lim Siew Chin, my beloved companion of 43 years. Your constant support and loving rebukes are without count and measure!

In and around everything and everyone, I acknowledge the transforming work of the eternal living Voice, Word, and Spirit of Yeshua ha Mashiach, Jesus the Christ, who makes us free and transforms us as we continue in his teachings.

FREE Bonus Offers
Worth over $550 for YOU

This workbook can't contain all that needs to be said, or what I want to say, or what is relevant to you at this time. I encourage you to continue with action at every stage, in every chapter.

So, I've included these wonderful FREE offers for you. Don't miss out: act TODAY.

By going to my website or using the QR code below, or emailing me, you will get access to:

- ✓ Up to 30-minutes online or by phone with me, completely obligation free, regarding the issues you or your group are working through right now. Given modern technology, this can be from anywhere in the world.

- ✓ A digital download of an incredible bonus chapter that includes (a) stories of how some of the book's questions or challenges are working out in my situations, and (b) what it can mean to walk with one another through transforming trauma one-to-one, or in families, teams and organisations over many years if necessary. This chapter is not available anywhere else.

- ✓ Three months of weekly e-classes based on this book.

I'd be delighted to continue conversations with you about any topic or thread of interest from this book.

Contact me via hello@transformingtraumatogether.com
my website www.neilhockey.com
or just scan this QR code

Live Passionately
  Think Deeply
    for Lasting Change!

CONTENTS

Foreword		1
Introduction – Why Truth Matters to Us (at) All		3
Part 1 – Examine Taboo Trauma's Roots		9
Chapter 1	**Intuit Trauma's Journey into Truth**	11
	A personal journey in negotiating taboo trauma	13
	Roots in domestic, political and colonial violence call for truth-telling	15
	Discern THE SPECS for truth – a challenge in wholistic analysis	16
	Take up the challenge – discern pathways to growth	18
Chapter 2	**People, Persuasion or Propaganda: Whose Truth Might we Trust?**	23
	Search out reliable sources of truth: your growing years	24
	Question voices of authority – but how?	26
	Move to strategic questioning	28
	Acknowledge multigenerational legacies	29
Chapter 3	**Collectively Cultivate Hope's Roots (for Trust and Love)**	35
	Pursuing truth through radical-conservative faith relationships	37
	Step #1: Disarm trauma's triggers through T.R.A.U.M.A.	39
	Step #2: Hold uppermost 4 assumptions	41
	Step #3: Consistently apply 6 principles	42
Part 2 – Regenerate Integrity		47
Chapter 4	**Get Clear on Your Journey: Trust Betrayed?**	49
	A personal journey in learning to trust and be trustworthy	51
	Define integrity, trust and love	53
	Discern truth as a basis for hope through facing realities	56
	Regain control in life – develop insight especially within suffering	58
Chapter 5	**Matters of T.R.U.T.H. – Go Deeper as Hope Spirals**	63
	Prioritise collective and personal integrity	64
	Explain truth in practice – but how?	65
	Deepen your spiral of hope through T.R.U.T.H.	68
	Against post-truth? Get back to basic structures!	71

Chapter 6	Regenerate Identity and Integrity Through Truth	77
	Distinguish lawful from legal: an aid in navigating post-truth	79
	Truth is being questioned in the Dock – an Indigenous perspective	79
	Reflect on a king's coronation in history – deeply challenging national integrity?	82
	Engage truth, restore identity, regenerate integrity – grieving's hard roads	84

Part 3 – Sustain Collective Integrity: Make Change a Habit!   91

Chapter 7	Restore Trust, Pursue Truth	93
	A personal journey in consolidating trust for sustainable integrity	94
	Acknowledge your hope fluctuating over time	96
	Learn from trauma in tribal north-east India	97
	Celebrate your own Nagod – an 'insignificant' town in central India	99

Chapter 8	Making Truth MATTers Entirely Pervade You	103
	Sustain integrity through life's inevitable rhythms – but how?	104
	Live life to the full at Micro, Macro and Meta levels	105
	Develop habitual Actions and in-Actions	108
	Become Transformed, Transformative and Trustworthy people – grounded through Totalising, Transformist and Transitional praxis	108

Chapter 9	Let Truth MattERS Guide You through Esteem to Wholistic Wellbeing	117
	Sustain and extend yourselves through deep thinking and deep working	119
	Build from the deep – your web of 7 'E's from Esteem to Eudaimonia	120
	Be Reflexive throughout your web – balance your social relationships with social concerns	125
	Strengthen every Self among yourselves	127

Chapter 10	Now What?	133
	Where is your fallow ground?	134
	Your next step?	139

Recommended Reading List	**141**
Resources	**149**
About the Author	**153**

FOREWORD

I have known Dr Neil Hockey since he was an under-graduate student at The University of Queensland and have remained in contact with him up to the present. Over this long period, I have been struck by his deeply caring values, his educational and entrepreneurial abilities, his passion for justice and well-being and his amazing ability to "hang-in" in both good and difficult times.

There are those who have, over much of their life, identified with Indigenous communities, seeking to work cooperatively with them to bring about well-being and human flourishing. Neil is one such person. I am aware of his family's deep connection with Indigenous communities, his work in India and then in Australia, particularly in the Logan-Beaudesert region.

Several years ago, Neil gave a public talk of his work at the Crown Hotel in Brisbane. This talk was so well received that it was subsequently published in *Pub Theology: Where Potato Wedges and a Beer are a Eucharistic Experience* (Manchester, UK: Piquant Editions, 2021) under the title: "A Journey in Fragile Solidarity". On reading this I was struck, once again, by the deep and long-lasting commitment he has made in relation to Indigenous education, job creation and community welfare. And undoubtedly there was so much more he accomplished that I know nothing about.

Neil is a deeply reflective practitioner. The scope of this work *Transforming Trauma Together* is monumental. Community development mingles with advocacy and justice issues; joins with community building, counselling and spiritual formation; is linked to teaching, mentoring and writing. The personal, the communal and the global are all at play. Enabling, formation, empowerment move one to the beauty of well-being, human flourishing and transformation. This profound visionary workbook when embodied in love and sacrificial deeds can be the harbinger of much needed change.

Dr Charles Ringma
charlesringma.com

Prof. Charles Ringma, AM, PhD, TSSF is Emeritus Prof. Regent College, Vancouver and Research Prof. Asian Theological Seminary, Metro Manila. His latest book is *In the Midst of Much-Doing: Cultivating a Missional Spirituality.*

INTRODUCTION
Why Truth Matters to Us (at) All

Wherever I've lived and worked I have somehow become involved with people affected by trauma in ways big or small, or at the very least, people who like all of us sometimes seem plagued by uncertainty or confusion, especially in recent times.

Over decades and under others' guidance with prayer, I've worked consistently at resolving some contradictions in my own life.

I've also studied a lot of psychology and different ways of counselling, yet I'm not a qualified psychologist nor am I an official counsellor, but I *have* found that by **working together in** our families, teams and any small group **alongside** the professionally trained, we can make a lot of progress over time.

Listening to each other's stories, asking strategic questions and sharing insights, knowledge, understanding and skills, can be a great step towards resolving, or at least transforming, some effects of trauma.

> *Where there is no wise counsel and intelligent guidance, the people collapse and fall. But with a multitude of such counsellors there is strength.*
>
> **Proverbs 11:14**

My trauma expertise comes from direct personal and community work experience, living in therapeutic communities and ongoing research alongside other lovers of this way. This book is my proposed outline of what we must do to reach and sustain the outcomes we strive for every day.

It's a struggle, a tough yet exhilarating journey to be faithful to our chosen values. My own journey of growing through trauma began when I started to notice traits and patterns of behaviour in myself, extended family members and close friends.

Seeing these patterns recurring over time, some of us began to talk about them. We saw that if we began to face the truth of ourselves, our histories and our situations, and then act on that truth, there were powerful implications for our identities, our sense of worth and our work.

This book invites all readers then to focus on Transforming Trauma **Together**, to learn to grow through trauma by doing the hard work of strengthening trust while re-awakening and rebuilding hope. In essence it's quite simple, but we must also discern the truth of what helps us to change and what hinders, including trauma endured both past and present.

Truth? A lot of academics and others throughout the population today assert there is no such thing as truth. If that were the case, then there'd be no such thing as lies, leaving our life together on shaky grounds. That's why this book calls you to commit to ***thinking, living*** and ***speaking truth***.

The world is constantly changing. For many the main goal might simply be to survive. Educators or other leaders in the human services sector (including family and community leaders) strive for personal, social or corporate transformation, but the uncertainty, confusion and to varying degrees trauma (often not acknowledged) can render some key outcomes unsustainable.

Have **you** felt disheartened recently? I certainly have. There are sharp declines globally in mental health among both young and old. I recently had published a chapter on sustaining the spirit of ourselves, our work and the Spirit through whom we live and work. Many writers summarise some worst possible scenarios facing humanity.

We're engulfed by crises in health, in education and in food and fuel shortages, with wars and conflicts escalating. We're swamped daily with news of climate events resulting in part from human activity. (The kinds of human activity and the fraction they contribute are contested).

Who is this book for then?

If you, your family, friends, or associates are a little **confused, concerned** or **traumatised** then this book is for you.

If you **struggle to maintain hope** each day, if you find it **just a little harder to trust** people you used to trust, then this book is for you.

If there are **friends or family** members who **now seem a bit estranged** and you long to recover some of that camaraderie or commitment to a set of common goals, then this book just might be for you, **whether you are eighteen or eighty**.

The whole book introduces you to my life of pursuing truth. It summarises my journey shared with many. It's also my invitation to further conversation, by emailing hello@transformingtraumatogether.com or via www.neilhockey.com.

Readers could initially fall into one or more of the following categories:

1. **Those I've shared life with deeply at times** over many decades. These include my extended families in Australia and Malaysia. They also include close friends from **different faith communities** in several countries.

2. Workers in non-government organisations (NGOs) and Government Departments, especially **in the fields of education or health**, or those **working with traumatised people and communities**.

3. People in **recognised positions of leadership** across many sectors (including family life). All leaders acknowledge the reality of **struggling to maintain outcomes long-term**.

Common to all readers will be their experience in what will be a lifelong challenge: **keeping a balance between** three main priorities in life:

- ➢ **family** commitments or loyalties
- ➢ **beliefs** or cultural values
- ➢ **work** roles and responsibilities.

Throughout my extended families, everywhere I've been, and everywhere I've worked, it's clear there will at times be tensions between these same commitments or convictions, especially when they overlap as in family businesses or community organisations.

Overview

The three parts of this book cover issues of trauma, integrity and transformation.

First, in enduring our own or others' trauma we might unearth taboos while cultivating collective roots of hope, trust and love. Chapters 1-3 draw mainly from **my own journey**.

Second, in our striving to rebuild trust arising from rekindled hope, we need to regenerate our sense of integrity or wholeness. Chapters 4-6 recount learnings from **journeying with Indigenous friends**.

Third, by embedding trust in relationships with our families, friends, and wider connections, we need to work towards sustaining this transformative rhythm and thus our collective integrity in the long term. Chapters 7-9 focus more on **Asian contexts**.

I'll be drawing from my own and friends' experiences, thoughts and writings. In addition to my earliest and ongoing experiences of family; I'm privileged to be sharing life with Australian Goories or Indigenous families and groups and with friends and co-workers across Australia, India and Malaysia. Underpinning it all is my worldview as shaped by being brought up in a world where biblical writings, teaching and practice permeated everything we said or did.

Now for some readers that could be a turn-off. I also went through phases where I questioned and doubted elements of foundational teachings. However, doubts and questions are my friends in many places where I'm surrounded by questioners from other faiths too. That's our common ground – **grappling with uncertainty as we pursue truth**. It stands us in good stead.

So, each of the three parts is introduced by a personal story which then blends into a sequence of:

- expanding that theme with other stories to illustrate key points
- insights on trauma, truth or transformation, with challenges to put into action
- an outline of how I'm seeing those challenges being partially met in my own journey

Every chapter is written as a continuous process building on what came before. Each chapter is your call to action.

I hope to **sit**, **walk** and eventually **work with you** in that gap of knowledge and way of living. I hope to inspire you, starting from what you *do* know, leading through what you *don't* know, to what you *could* know and then helping put that into practice.

Let's carefully build inspiring, sustainable bridges!

PART 1
Examine Taboo Trauma's Roots

We all want to improve and flourish. On the one hand this assumes we know what's right, just, safe, good, trustworthy and true! On the other hand, we've all been hurt, frustrated or distressed either directly or indirectly when confronted by injustice or deception.

Part 1 invites you to:

- ✓ **engage possible taboos**
- ✓ **confront calls for truth-telling**
- ✓ and **respond personally**.

Chapter 1 reflects on domestic and political trauma with some focus on our Australian families, teams and organisations.

Chapter 2 asks whose truth might we trust amid persuasion and propaganda.

Chapter 3 challenges us to collectively cultivate hope's roots with six key actions, building on appropriate assumptions and principles to foster growing **through** trauma.

I don't intend to re-traumatise you by possibly evoking experiences of trauma. I do want to help facilitate your journey along with others towards embracing a more complete range of emotions, experiences and commitments.

CHAPTER 1

Intuit Trauma's Journey into Truth

*"Many times, trauma in a person
decontextualised over time
can look like personality.
Trauma in a family
decontextualised over time can look like
family traits,
trauma decontextualised in a people
over time can look like culture
and it takes time
to slow it down
so you can begin to discern what's what."*

Resmaa Menakem

CHAPTER 1
Intuit Trauma's Journey into Truth

> The nature of trauma is that you don't want to **relive** it.
> You don't want to **have** the trauma.
> You don't want to **talk** about the trauma.
> You don't want to **revisit** it and will put up every possible **barrier** to re-traumatizing.
> You can call that **resistance**, but I would call that a healthy way of trying to **cope**.
>
> **Bessel van der Kolk MD (NICABM**)

An Indigenous community worker colleague once asked me, "What keeps you going, you always seem so centred and calm?" I wasn't so sure. There's many a day I don't feel that way!

He continued, "How do you keep grappling with the same community issues, pushing against walls that never seem to yield, day after day, year after year?"

I know that even when I **do see real changes** in situations or feel that we've achieved some great goals, the challenge follows:

How can we now sustain those outcomes?

It often seems there's something just waiting to trip us up just when we think we're making progress. Roots of some triggers go way back for me.

Chapter 1: Intuit Trauma's Journey into Truth

A personal journey in negotiating taboo trauma

As a toddler, I was the fifth child. At my cousins' home I remember one time very well in a sequence of flashbacks:

- ➤ wetting the bed
- ➤ standing watching my uncle making me a wooden toy
- ➤ my cousins offering my 4year-old sister some "jellybeans" from a bush on the side of the road and laughing as she sputtered and spat from eating a fiery hot chilli.

It was my first time away from my parents overnight.
It must have been for a few nights.
I was 30 months old.
It was winter.

Then my sister and I went back home. I wasn't consciously aware of things being different. It took decades to come to know let alone grasp fully the significance of that homecoming and the years that followed. It was meant to be a time of great joy. My dad had long talked of having six children – three boys and three girls. I was the third son with two girls separating me from the older boys. The sixth child born that week was indeed a beautiful little girl, but … she was stillborn.

The culture was different back then.
Today parents are encouraged to spend precious time in physical contact with their baby, grieving together and preparing the funeral.
Not so then.

Our parents' daughter and our sister, named but unknown, was literally snatched from the womb and disposed of. My parents were not allowed to see, let alone touch or admire the now departing fruit of their labour.

Somehow in keeping with this culture of silence the entire matter of our absent sister was from that time on a taboo subject. Each family member developed their own ways of dealing with the absence, of working through the grief, alone. It certainly affected our family dynamics permanently even as when adults and parents we came to piece together the story of what had happened.

My own experience of trauma is small compared to that of others. I share it because it shows how family, social and organisational life can be impacted by avoiding truth.

Trauma is real. Its effects are real.

On the one hand it can be insidious. Trauma tends to be covered by webs of denial. Long-term patterns of deception arise even within relationships we thought were grounded in mutual trust, or there can be outbursts of anger that seem to spring out of nowhere. All these observable behaviours are in fact often very deep-rooted. Might these negative patterns be minimised or even largely eradicated?

On the other hand, past trauma can be helpful, warning us of personal or wider threats to be resisted. For example, we instinctively tend to know when something doesn't ring true. Especially at such times, **we need to take responsibility** for our **lingering thoughts, words** and **actions**.

I've had to learn this lesson from a lifetime's living with consequences of trauma that was rarely if ever discussed. I'm talking of more than the loss of my stillborn sister. Let me explain.

Since my teens I've lived and worked among families and communities fractured by some form or another of domestic, family, or social violence. I believed this was due to my growing concern for justice. I then began to suspect that subconsciously it was partly because my own upbringing was a bit that way inclined also.

As a family we were always very close to our **father's mother**, our paternal grandmother, but I only ever remember seeing my **father's father** for a few minutes, maybe three times as a child. His infidelity decades earlier estranged his entire family. He neglected them for life. Consequently, my father took on major responsibilities as a 12yo in a 1930s family.

My **mother's** parents were different. They had emigrated from London's lower east-end in 1912, and as children we saw them regularly. Then they moved in with us for their final years. We relish those good memories.

Decades earlier however, this grandfather tended to get violent, sometimes subtle, but at times explosive. That left some scars on his five sons and daughter, our mother. Such effects can linger for generations. They can also compound throughout society.

Roots in domestic, political and colonial violence call for truth-telling

Families, communities and nations are under increasing stress. How might we find ways forward through what are for many, the mists of trauma? Both root causes and consequences must be identified before we can begin to deal with them.

Escalating, reverberating across all levels of Australian society are calls for truth-telling in relation to ongoing harassment and abuse of women and girls particularly. This follows years of increasing calls for urgent action regarding the scale of **Australian domestic violence**. The rate of gender-violence is horrific, averaging almost two deaths per week in 2024 (as of June). One in every four girls are said to have been abused sexually, and one in seven boys.

There are challenges for men and boys to change their behaviour. Some women too are implicated in this rising crescendo. According to most recent studies, 23% of women reported experiencing violence at the hands of an intimate partner, as well as 7.8% of men.

Politically, parliaments' hallowed halls are also implicated. Early in 2021 several allegations involving rape and other sexual misconduct against women were raised. Regarding those allegations, the relevant Wikipedia article (see the resources list for this chapter) also details a series of similar situations in previous years.

This is contemporary Australia. Widespread family violence, harassment and abuse, from private homes to TV broadcasters to parliaments all call for truth-telling and a widespread clean out. Globally there have been increasing calls for truth-telling in relation to **colonial history**. We've all observed and absorbed impacts of these national and global trends. It's recognised that entire cultures, entire ways of being, living and working need close examination. So too do their associated social, political and economic structures.

As we can see the challenge is vast!

Discern THE SPECS for truth – a challenge in wholistic analysis

Every story, every emerging crisis either implies or explicitly states a range of issues including how trauma is generated and its consequences. I've struggled to think through how we can discern the full reality and respond together. Then I came up with an acronym.

In referring to building a house, product or device we can ask, "What's the specifications?" or just casually "What's **THE SPECS**?" I've chosen to use this question as an acronym to help me grapple with problems like domestic or family violence, racism, suicides, crime rates, wider conflicts and wars. It applies also to "natural" crises such as climate

Chapter 1: Intuit Trauma's Journey into Truth

change or pandemics and how governments and societies respond to these.

In every case many perspectives must be considered together to discern what is right, just, and true:

T – Theology every person or group holds to a faith system – whether belief in one God, many gods, no gods, we are all gods or part of a universal Spirit or Consciousness.

H – History there is nothing new under the sun, everything and everyone has roots in the past.

E – Economics follow the money trails, although not many want to!

S – Science follow "the Science", as everyone is urged to.

P – Philosophy love the wisdom of truth, beauty and goodness (these depend on the values you strengthen through your choices).

E – Ecology this is the totality or pattern of relations between organisms and their environment.

C – Culture all the arts, values, beliefs, customs, institutions plus other human products are considered together as a whole.

S – Social Science add to history, economics and the **natural** sciences above, other **social** ones, such as geography, sociology, psychology, anthropology, political science etc.

That sounds like a lot of work, but we succeed by working together.

Take up the challenge – discern pathways to growth

A similar approach is called **Systems Thinking** where all the different, confusing, disconnected parts of life, of problems or situations, are seen as interdependent parts of a whole. People taking up this approach include:

- Students
- Teachers
- Other professionals
- Businesses
- Governments
- Groups like the World Economic Forum.

You might wonder why I've separated History and Economics from other Sciences in my approach to "THE SPECS" above?

First, it seems that discussion, debate and policies around many issues in the 21st century seem to ignore or at best minimise the **historical context** of that issue. It's like the only lesson we learn from history is that we rarely learn anything from history!

Second, economics as money and financial systems seems to dominate most decisions and policy directions in our day and age. It's the hidden curriculum. Didn't someone once say, "You can't serve both God and Mammon"? (Mammon means wealth.)

In my own thinking, I apply the above acronym to prime examples like modern day "fights for freedom": current conflicts in Ukraine, Africa, the Middle East or to climate crises and pandemics.

Chapter 1: Intuit Trauma's Journey into Truth

> **These topics are too big** for this book.
> I prefer to **workshop responses** in depth **with your group**.

It is precisely crises and conflicts like the Middle East that dominate our media channels, often our personal social media and our national consciousness in many countries. Each country tends to (at least publicly) support one side or another in a conflict, depending on their mix of elements in "THE SPECS".

Caught in the middle are populations in general like local Australian schools and their communities which have growing numbers of migrants or refugees from across the world. It's these global conflicts and crises that seep into our consciousness and add to confusion, uncertainty and a growing sense of trauma.

How can these become our friends by setting us on a path to search out truth, wisdom and appropriate action? Summarising some definitions of trauma helps here:

a) Trauma is not a flaw or a weakness, but the body's protective response to an event – or a series of events – that it perceives as potentially dangerous.

b) Trauma is the response to a deeply distressing or disturbing event that
   - overwhelms an individual's ability to cope
   - causes feelings of helplessness
   - diminishes their sense of self, and/or
   - diminishes their ability to feel a **full** range of emotions and experiences.

c) Trauma is any encounter, acute or prolonged, that overwhelms the psyche's capacity to process the experience.

d) Trauma is too intense to hold, integrate or comprehend, saturating our capacity to make sense of the experience.

It's when we don't have a space, environment and people capable of supporting us that traumatic experiences are generated. Remember pain itself is not necessarily traumatic but pain that is not witnessed is far more likely to be. We feel overwhelmed and alone in our apprenticeship with sorrow.

> *There is more and more evidence that dissociation is caused by dysfunctional attachment – you don't have somebody who looks at you and picks you up and responds to you when you are in distress, so you learn to deal with your misery by shutting yourself down.*
>
> **Bessel van der Kolk, MD (NICABM)**

No-one can live their entire lives without being impacted by trauma. As part of human existence, it can never be avoided completely.

For further reading check the relevant links for **Chapter 1** in the **Recommended Reading List**.

Chapter 1: Intuit Trauma's Journey into Truth

Suggestions for Action now

Think about times when you struggled with words or actions (your own or others) that somehow didn't seem quite right, when something made you uneasy.

What about those times when you felt disturbed or angry about how you or others were treated? For example:

1. a parent, partner, child or other relative
2. a colleague, your employer or some politician
3. a journalist, media spokesperson or someone on social media
4. representatives from various sectors, e.g. education, health, business, other non-government etc.
5. international or global crises, of which there are many!

Most of the time our responses to events or circumstances around us are just normal human reactions appropriate to what's happening.

Take time now to **focus on at least one specific experience of trauma** as described above, whether **yours or someone else's**. **What might it take** for you and/or others to **set up** or **join a space** to **work together** into the future?

Life's challenge is to use confusion or trauma not as an excuse to withdraw from others but a gateway to deepen our trust in each other!

So

1. Face the fact that a life lived well includes negotiating trauma.
2. If our journeys are about learning to trust they are also about learning to be trustworthy.
3. If our daily patterns of life are to be sustainable in the long-term, they must be filled with little acts of building trust.

We need to **work together** at growing through these experiences over the months, years, and decades of our lives, towards re-igniting and rebuilding a spiral of hope, trust and love that is unrelenting.

How then, and with whom? Just who can you trust?

CHAPTER 2

People, Persuasion or Propaganda: Whose Truth Might We Trust?

*"It takes a lifetime to fully come to grips
with a moral and ethical framework
that is sustainable and internally consistent
for us, our families,
and the entire network of people in our lives."*

Neil Hockey

CHAPTER 2

People, Persuasion or Propaganda:
Whose Truth Might We Trust?

> *If you want to run fast, run alone.*
> *If you want to run far, run together.*
> **An African proverb (most likely)**
>
> *You alone can do it, but you cannot do it alone.*
> **Dave Andrews**

We're created for connection. However, building and re-building trust in yourselves and in others can't be self-centred. Who might you build with then?

> How might we discern trustworthy sources of truth
> when confusion, stress, conflict and trauma are increasing?

Search out reliable sources of truth: your growing years

I grew up in what could be called a radical-conservative faith-based extended family. Radicals are generally seen as wanting to change society even to the extent of making other people really upset! Conservatives are thought to be committed to keeping things the same. That too can upset other people!

Chapter 2: People, Persuasion or Propaganda: Whose Truth Might We Trust?

Why then do I describe my family life as being both radical *and* conservative? Furthermore, what on earth might a heavenly faith have to do with all that? I'll explain more in Chapter 3. Here I relate my search for reliable sources of truth while subconsciously negotiating a taboo trauma.

I was quiet and introspective as the youngest child. This began to change though. We lived on a dirt-road slope where all the local kids rode their home-made go-carts downhill. Our neighbourhood was dynamic and boisterous, playing cricket uphill on the wide grassy footpaths. Moreover, our enthusiastic and highly active church youth group consolidated a good springboard for life. We were socially aware, committed, and striving to relate our beliefs to our experience of the world.

Then at university I decided that if my faith and spirituality were to be relevant, they had to be so for the whole of life, in all of work in the world, and amongst people of all cultures. This became a manifesto for the largest Christian group (around 200 members) on the University of Queensland campus by my third year of university. I became president of that group.

Lunchtime debates used to take place regularly between representatives of this group (the Evangelical Union) and those of another who I remember as the libertarian communists (the Self-Management Group). One key point of contention was **the ultimate source of humanity's ills**. Is it alienation from God (evidenced by alienation from self, each other, society, and the environment)? Or if we could leave "God" out of the equation, is it the fact that we don't take control of our own lives?

These two options have remained uppermost in my thinking for the past five decades. I now see that the two must be held in tension. The issue of trust is central to both questions.

Question voices of authority – but how?

What might be a rational basis for trusting a God? Conversely how serious are we in arguing that we can trust ourselves and the rest of humanity to control our own lives? What examples might history provide?

It was an era fuelled by global upheavals. Families were breaking up. God too seemed dead. There was Watergate, protracted wars, and the threat of nuclear annihilation.

The Vietnam War was moving towards a climax. This tended to overshadow other protests, for example those on issues raised by Aboriginal activists such as Denis Walker. All student activists became restricted by universities moving towards continuous assessment instead of just annual exams. As students we became repulsed by war's insanity. Inspired by writers such as Art Gish, Jacques Ellul and Gene Sharp, many of us were seriously questioning whether violence could bring about radical social and political transformation.

We determined instead to build communities of people committed to being transformed themselves, also becoming a transforming influence for good. We began by developing a small network of community houses in the suburbs surrounding the university. These households grew to be hubs of hope, healing and recovery for many young people impacted by trauma.

Getting together daily and weekly was top priority. There were passionate discussions, debates and prayer. We explored examples from history where personal, social, and political changes had stood the test of years. So, crucial to any argument were matters of truth, hope and trust.

Chapter 2: People, Persuasion or Propaganda: Whose Truth Might We Trust?

This trauma → community, and truth → transformation scenario became one template for my life's journey.

I completed four years of campus and student-community life in the mid-70s. At university we had great ideals, but living out our ideals in the big wider world could be a shock to the system! Wherever I went I not only began to learn some hard lessons in trusting others' words and actions, I also began to look inside myself more deeply. How trustworthy am I in all my relationships with family, friends and work colleagues?

My next 17 years began and ended with school teaching, initially in the plains of rural Queensland then later, a boarding school in the mountains of South India. In between were six years helping establish therapeutic communities in North India, those of New Delhi's Sahara House plus related urban and rural sites. These teams struggled to survive themselves. We were all in our 20s and 30s, sharing our homes and entire lives with people battling a whole lot of addictive behaviours – their responses to relentless injustice and oppression. **Over forty years later** many of those community residents **continue to serve sacrificially**.

Having married into a Chinese Malaysian family and visiting there often, I relish maintaining contact with some friends in the region. Wherever I go, together we often ask:

> Amid many voices
> how can we have confidence
> in our sources of authority?

Since childhood I've been interacting with and observing world-impacting leaders. For some their impact is, or has been, limited by immature thinking and wilful wrongdoing. I can only wonder what unresolved trauma might have contributed to such limitations. I conclude that till the day we die we'll all still be tempted to satisfy our own selfish desires, to others' detriment.

In the process we might be subjected to others' manipulation and control, to our own detriment and potentially to others' also.

Move to Strategic Questioning

Over everyone's lifetime there are those whose integrity we would question, some of whom we know personally. Even as children we can often sense intuitively those we see as less trustworthy. Then we learn to discuss these issues rationally as we grow. I hope so!

Over time I grew to discern more carefully which leaders seemed trustworthy (or not) in all spheres of life. They've impacted me as a young adult in early employment and as an adult in very diverse contexts across three countries. Who then might we trust?

Are we engaging with persuasive argument or **falling foul** of propaganda? What are our options when we lose trust in our leadership because of what they say, what they do, or don't do, especially when those leaders get to remain in their positions while those with seemingly better leadership potential leave the group in frustration or are pushed out?

There are some workplaces where that can be traumatising, even relentlessly so. During periods of relief-teaching I've worked in many "tough" schools. Most of the time you see many teachers who are welcoming, hard-working, and generally cheerful. There are also highly supportive administration staff, but not all the time.

Chapter 2: People, Persuasion or Propaganda: Whose Truth Might We Trust?

One school I worked at had become a refuge for several teachers from another school in the same district. That school's principal was (in one teacher's words) "such a psychopathic control freak" that all trust had dissipated, and those teachers had transferred out.

Tracy Tully was one state-school long-term principal who took a stand against a widespread toxic culture. In her book *"FEARless: Buckle Up ... Build Resilience"* she recounts corruption and workplace bullying not just by school staff, but education sector administration also. Such experiences are also backed up by **Peter Coaldrake's scathing report** into the Queensland state's public sector in 2022.

My question is, what can we do in similar seemingly intolerable circumstances to feed a spiral of hope within, for it's said that without hope we can't live more than seconds.
Hope is critical, especially when we feel neglected, abused, or even abandoned. Many today in increasing numbers have such experiences.

In Chapter 3 I'll be elaborating some actions I've found to be essential to re-kindling and fanning a spiral of hope and trust. For myself it's taken years, even decades, to more fully understand and work through these processes. I'll outline how these apply in my life. My final point for Chapter 2 however is to note trauma's complexity for many.

Acknowledge multi-generational legacies

Richard Trudgen is a community worker serving alongside Yolŋu in the Northern Territory for over 50 years. In his community-inspired and directed book *"Why Warriors Lie Down and Die"* he explains the transmission of trauma from any one generation to those that follow.

He concludes by observing that powerful, fearless, extremely mature, and intelligent Yolŋu leaders were struggling. They seemed powerless when confronted with what was from their cultural and historical perspective, the aggressive, lawless, and meaningless actions of Balanda (whitefellas).

Judy Atkinson is the author of *"Trauma Trails, Recreating Song Lines: The transgenerational effects of trauma in Indigenous Australia"*. Her participatory research with a small group helps provide ground-breaking answers to the questions of how to solve problems of cross-generational trauma. *"Trauma Trails"* moves beyond the rhetoric of victimhood. It provides inspiration for anyone concerned about both Indigenous and non-Indigenous communities today. I return to this issue in Part 2. The emphasis in Part 1 is on our need to cultivate roots of hope, trust and love by:

- ✓ taking time and effort
- ✓ acting patiently and persistently
- ✓ working together.

Chapter 2: People, Persuasion or Propaganda: Whose Truth Might We Trust?

Chapter Summary

This chapter's challenge was to discern trustworthy sources of truth when surrounded by trauma. The temptation we all face is to:

- **walk away** from stressful situations,
- **withdraw** from pain,
- **reject** a host of options for strength and hope,
- **turn inwards** to our own private social group.

In Chapters 1 and 2 **I've advocated instead**, that however small or large our immediate source of comfort is, we'll benefit greatly by working with others to:

- **face the reality** of past or present trauma
- **confidently identify** some root causes
- **put aside** what we can from the past
- **enjoy**, or **at least endure**, the present.

I've noted that there'll always be limits to the degree of confidence we can have in others. Over time we get to know more of each person's naturally flawed character, their contradictory words and confusing actions. Quite rightly, we overlook their faults a lot of the time, but we must learn to glean aspects of truth from what we observe.

I've shared parts of my own journey:
a gradual move
from simply questioning life around me
to asking open-ended, strategic questions in pursuit of truth and flourishing!

Whether you're fifteen or fifty
you might see yourself
in there
somewhere.

I've identified some kinds of struggles we might all have
in gaining confidence
to discern truth.

You can be sure it's there
somewhere
amid the great diversity of seemingly authoritative voices clamouring
for our attention.

I've introduced a reality that people most traumatised are likely suffering from multi-generational legacies of trauma, with more on that to come.

There's no way I could have written this book ten or twenty years ago. I lacked a level of maturity that comes with extended life experience. I'd not yet gained the insights I now possess. Even five years ago, I was nowhere near a state of equilibrium in my life that would allow me enough emotional space to reflect more fully and so articulate the bigger picture.

Time passes by.
Life's experiences grow more diverse and complex.
It's all teaching me patience in working through impacts of my own minor trauma.

More importantly, it requires patience with others.

> For further reading check the relevant links for **Chapter 2**
> in the **Recommended Reading List**.

Chapter 2: People, Persuasion or Propaganda: Whose Truth Might We Trust?

Suggestions for Action now

Take time writing responses to the following:

1. List three of the most stressful times in your life so far.

2. How did you respond in each situation, or over time if the stress continued as it can for years?

3. What is causing you the greatest stress in your life this year?

4. List at least two or three people you're most likely to talk with about these issues.

    Meet with them in a place suitable for everyone and get started.

5. Make sure everyone in the group is familiar with Chapters 1 and 2 as far as possible.

6. Have each person share their responses to the questions above.

7. Now ask strategic questions of each other, as to how you might move into the future with patient hope, trusting faithfulness and unconditional love.

The seven steps above will help prepare you for engaging Parts 2 and 3 of *Transforming Trauma Together*. First though, Chapter 3 will conclude Part 1. It outlines approaches or practical steps we can all take to discern truth in the process of transforming trauma and so overcoming some of its consequences.

CHAPTER 3

Collectively Cultivate Hope's Roots (for Trust and Love)

*"We can't thrive without trust and much love.
However, we must start with ourselves."*

Neil Hockey

CHAPTER 3
*Collectively Cultivate Hope's Roots
(for Trust and Love)*

This chapter suggests ways we can begin resolving chapter 2's challenge when overwhelmed by stress or trauma, alone and with others.

It helps to get down to the facts of a matter, but can you trust your sources? **Earlier** generations in Western countries tended to claim the Bible as a primary source. **Recently**, a Catholic church representative claimed that people tend to **refer to one or more** of **three categories as sources of authority:**

1. their own powers of reasoning
2. the Bible
3. their church traditions.

Of course, agnostics or atheists with **no faith** might claim their powers of reasoning are **un-biased** and so stronger, while those from **other faith-communities** such as Buddhists, Hindus, Muslims, animists, etc., have their own oral traditions, writings, cultural practices, and ways of reasoning developed over time.

Today on the one hand many Western believers are deconstructing their biblical faith. Others are turning to other faiths. **On the other hand,** many more in non-Western countries are turning not only to faith **in** the Bible but in the Christ **of** the Bible, often under traumatising circumstances. I'm starting then from two premises:

Chapter 3: Collectively Cultivate Hope's Roots (for Trust and Love)

1. Faith, doubt, apathy or opposition are **common factors** across all cultures.
2. **Contemporary** uncertainties, confusion or trauma **tend to be complex** whether in the East or West, North or South amid military conflicts and health crises.

Pursuing truth through radical-conservative faith relationships

As kids growing up there were certainly aspects of "church" that seemed conservative, especially as we began to experience more of the world. We thought "the faith of our fathers" was a bit constrictive, especially regarding women's roles. Both my home and church life however were in many respects:

1. **Participatory** – in theory anyone and everyone (particularly in public meetings if you were male) was encouraged to contribute.
2. **Collective** – facilitated or overseen by a genuinely non-hierarchical leadership (in contrast to many groups, churches, organisations, or companies today).
3. **Autonomous** yet **interdependent** – there was regular communication, interaction, mutual support, and encouragement between groups.

Then over the years I delved deeper into the historical roots of our "Open Brethren" movement. I discovered that within 1800s England it was indeed radical:

- ✓ It broke through many walls around institutional churches of its day.
- ✓ Like many before it this movement spawned leaders who joined others in pursuing truth, righteousness, and justice for the poor at home and beyond, throughout Europe, the Middle East, and across parts of Asia.

- ✓ Moreover, leaders within it traced their roots back through the centuries – a core meaning of the term radical.
- ✓ In terms of social justice theology, many simply lived out a radical submission to the call of Jesus.

Anthony Norris Groves is one great pioneering example as in a biography titled "Father of Faith Missions". Look it up at your leisure.

> Why do I include this brief historical backdrop?

First, history opens our minds to an **unlimited array** of lessons to be learnt.

Second, though lessons are unlimited, we need to have **a clear focus**. That focus for me is on the roots of my personal journey along the lines of my own tradition. I need to first walk the talk!

Third, my readers are from all sorts of faith- or non-faith families. It's up to you to apply any lessons to your own situation. However, as an author and speaker I must first critique, or **ask questions of, my own community of families**. I find there that even great leaders have their faults, weaknesses, and failures, impacted in part by traumatic circumstances.

Learning from history then I pose more strategic questions:

1. How might we **always be alert to** and **learn to defuse triggers of trauma?**
2. How might we **minimise impacts of long-term trauma** in our **families,** our **groups,** our **teams,** our **organisations?**

Chapter 3: Collectively Cultivate Hope's Roots (for Trust and Love)

and
3. What principles might best enable us to be **proactive** yet with **sensitivity** responding to needs, while **growing together** through multiple levels of stress or trauma **in our working for recovery?**

Hence the backdrop to this chapter is both general and personal in emphasising faith, doubt, and complexity.

From these three strategic questions I outline approaches or steps to discerning truth in the process of transforming trauma. Each step requires strengthening trust where we can within all our relationships. In Part 3 I'll relate more how they've worked out in my journey.

Each step builds on the previous one:

1. work personally on **6 goals**
2. hold uppermost **4 assumptions** that must underpin our caring
3. consistently apply **6 principles** to guide us in our caring.

Step #1: Disarm trauma's triggers through T.R.A.U.M.A.

I've developed this acronym to help me remember 6 goals in working on my own life. They're also actions or processes I issue as a call to leaders. We are all leaders in some way. This first step of working on your own inner and outer being, must be at the heart, the core of all you do, alone **and with others**. A modern term for these processes is self-regulation.

T – *Target* **your limbic system**, which stores all historical trauma in your body

Take a serious look at what's going on with your limbic system, the connections between your mind, heart, and body. So much has been written about this.

Begin your own research with a supportive group of friends!
    (Hint: start with my Recommended Readings for Chapter 3.)

R – *Reclaim* **your generational strengths**, a major source of countering trauma

Start writing up your genogram (your family tree with social patterns and psychological factors) to help you see the strengths (and weaknesses) of character in your own personal family generations (and others) who've gone before you. Reclaim the strengths!

A – *Activate* **and** *make actual* both yours and others' underlying values

Feed on the good values underpinning the actions of those who've gone before you.
Put them into practice more each day in your own situation.

U – *Understand* **yourself, others**, and any emerging patterns in behaviour

With understanding comes greater capacity to explain, but not to excuse. To explain is to identify potential triggers for healing and recovery.

M – *Maximise* **potentials**, both yours and others'

Strive to maximise all the potentials you see for positive change and growth.

Don't settle for mediocre.

Chapter 3: Collectively Cultivate Hope's Roots (for Trust and Love)

A – *Achieve* **and act on what you can**, don't focus on what you can't, right now

In acting towards your goals be content to achieve what you can, not worrying or over-stressing about what you can't, due to factors beyond your control.

The invitation is to somehow emerge from that place of being overwhelmed by confusion or trauma, finding your way through the mist or fog to grow and mature.

I must emphasise that I distilled **my first step** (TRAUMA) through **decades of community work**.

For the next two steps I've checked with professionals working in trauma recovery, for insights that resonate with my own praxis – habits I've built around my knowledge.

Step #2: Hold uppermost four assumptions

SAMHSA or *Substance Abuse and Mental Health Services Administration* is a branch of the US Department of Health and Human Services. This government agency is typical of many others when they emphasise that to deal effectively with trauma we must build on **four assumptions.**

The "Four R's":

1. **Realise** what trauma is and how it can affect people and groups
2. **Recognise** the signs of trauma
3. **Respond** to trauma by having an appropriate system of strategies, and
4. **Resist** re-traumatisation.

Thousands of organisations ground their work in similar assumptions. To minimise re-traumatising clients, they then shape all aspects of organisational growth and change around a set of six key principles as follows.

Step #3: Consistently apply 6 principles

1. **Safety** and **security** – physical, emotional and psychological
2. **Trustworthiness** and **transparency** – personal, in policies and procedures
3. **Peer support** – provide empathy, rapport and checking-in
4. **Collaboration** and **mutuality** – all stakeholders as self-regulating active partners
5. **Empowerment, voice,** and **choice** – cultivate ownership and self-determination
6. **Cultural** and **historical issues** – equal as people yet honouring the differences.

It's critical to create an environment that respects people's experience. Consequently, every member of your family, group, or team and every level of your organisation must remain open to ongoing change as they adapt to each other.

Chapter 3: Collectively Cultivate Hope's Roots (for Trust and Love)

Part 1 Summary

What are we to do in a beautiful world overcome with tragedy and trauma? We can't live without hope. We can't thrive without trust and much love. However, we must start with ourselves.

Everyone struggles with stress and trauma, whether their own or that of others. This book is my attempt to consolidate a sense of hope for the future, of trust in others along that journey and of courage in putting love into action. I believe it will do the same for you.

In Part 1 I first showed how confusion, uncertainty and trauma can be our friends when they **set us on a path to search out truth**. In our complex world this path will eventually lead us into THE SPECS for building hope. It's **a tapestry with many threads** which I outlined as:

Theology, **H**istory, **E**conomics, **S**cience, **P**hilosophy, **E**cology, **C**ulture, and **S**ocial Science.

That pathway to truth is clearly not possible without a measure of trust in one's own judgments, yet it can't lead to being self-centred. **That's where the challenge lies**. To discern with confidence calls for working together. It calls for patience. We can't give up hope especially when confronted by any multi-generational complexities. Trust must be strengthened over time within all our relationships, starting with oneself.

That's why I developed **Step #1** for my own daily reflections: the 6 proactive actions covered by the acronym TRAUMA. Then, in working further with others, discerning truth requires **Step #2**, the 4 Rs, and **Step #3**, the 6 principles.

Roots of any trauma tend to grow deeper sometimes when you experience rejection, mistrust, fear and competition.

Thankfully my growing understanding of personal and collective trauma helped me identify more with Indigenous families over the past 50 years. This is a major focus now in Part 2, Regenerating Integrity.

> For further reading check the relevant links for **Chapter 3** in the **Recommended Reading List**.

Chapter 3: Collectively Cultivate Hope's Roots (for Trust and Love)

Suggestions for Action now

Take some time to write a response to each of the following:

1. List three words or phrases to describe your home life, your experiences with social and cultural groups, including churches or other faith communities.

2. Discuss your responses with people in your trusted circle of family, friends or colleagues.

3. On a scale of 1-10, write down where you would assess yourself to be with each of the actions in Step #1, the TRAUMA spiral of self-regulation below.

T – **Target** your limbic system
R – **Reclaim** generational strengths
A – **Activate** and **actualise** underlying values
U – **Understand** patterns of behaviour in yourself, others and our society
M – **Maximise** all potentials
A – **Achieve** and enact what you can, not what you can't.

4. Take time to reflect on at least one group you meet with regularly. This can be family members, close friends, social group or work team for example. On a scale of 1-10, write down where you'd assess yourselves to be in **Step #2**, with each of the **four assumptions** that need to underpin any efforts to recover from trauma.

   Realise what trauma is and how it can affect people and groups
   Recognise the signs of trauma
   Respond to trauma by having an appropriate system of strategies, and
   Resist re-traumatising.

5. By yourself and then with others, reflect first on what you've observed or experienced as to how some groups have responded to traumatised people.

Pick one group or organisation, preferably your own. Rate it on a scale of 1-10, for each of the **6 principles** of **Step #3** that need to characterise any group working to support recovery from trauma:

1. **Safety** and **Security**
2. **Trustworthiness** and **Transparency**
3. **Peer Support**
4. **Collaboration** and **Mutuality**
5. **Empowerment, Voice,** and **Choice**
6. **Cultural** and **Historical issues**

Discuss with others, what such an organisation might do to improve their outcomes.

PART 2
Regenerate Integrity

In **Part 1** I drew lessons from my own journey:

> **First**, it's both possible and necessary that we each work through our own issues.
>
> **Second**, this journey to wholeness or integrity can't be taken alone.
>
> **Third**, it will take a lifetime with cycles of decay and regeneration along the way.

I've lived and worked alongside families of Indigenous descent at times over the past 40 years whether in Australia, India, or Malaysia. They teach me much from:

- their resilience over centuries
- their contributions to society whether forced or voluntary, and
- their massive potential to contribute even further to societies they now inhabit.

I've written many papers and two theses on these topics. There are numerous examples of Indigenous individuals, families and communities working collaboratively within their neighbourhoods or nations. Sadly, there are also many examples of trust being betrayed.

In **Part 2** I share glimpses of what I've learnt and am still learning.

Leading up to Australia's 2023 referendum on the Voice to Parliament and constitutional recognition of Indigenous peoples, central issues came to major public attention. One key theme was **collective integrity as a nation**. Simultaneously the same theme became prominent throughout Queen Elizabeth's passing and King Charles' coronation. Combining coronation and constitutional issues was a tumultuous mix. Advocates for either 'Yes' or 'No' were adamant that Australia's integrity as a nation was under threat, that trust would be further undermined throughout the country!

Chapter 4 focuses on this issue of trust so often betrayed. Yet if we commit relentlessly to discerning truth as reality, then to living it out daily it will unlock our trembling hearts and tentative hopes. This is my focus in **Chapter 5**. In **Chapter 6** – It's a long and hard road – restoring and strengthening identity over a lifetime through engaging truth and so regenerating integrity.

As I indicated on the back cover of this book, these three chapters together outline how to **be empowered** through patiently, persistently **rebuilding trust when struggling** with doubts, uncertainties and worry. They also give guidelines on how to **think** clearly and critically, **discern** truth and **be** free, **turning away** from personal and collective deceit for a **fuller, richer life.**

CHAPTER 4

Get Clear on Your Journey: Trust Betrayed?

"What the world needs now is love, sweet love!"

Hal David

CHAPTER 4
Get Clear on Your Journey: Trust Betrayed?

At the dawn of a new millennium in 2001, many writers reflected on our options: What role might reason, philosophy and the sciences play as we face an uncertain future? They see us living in both the best and worst of times. Simply put, as humans we both:

- **celebrate** and **fear** our differences
- **marvel at** and **distrust** science
- are unbelievably **affluent** and **poverty** stricken
- long for the **old** and enthuse over what is **new**.

We're simultaneously optimistic and pessimistic, brimming with hope yet plagued by fear. **How then** might we *live at peace,* while *making peace* through this storm?

From here on, use a lens that integrates Part 1.

> **First**, keep in mind not just reason, philosophy and the sciences, but **all THE SPECS** that form a flexible framework for working on any issue.
>
> **Second**, commit to my six steps, actions or processes engaging **TRAUMA**.
>
> **Third**, keep building on all **four Assumptions** embedded in the 4Rs.
>
> **Fourth**, apply daily all **six Principles** that can consistently guide and shape your caring for one another.

Chapter 4: Get Clear on Your Journey: Trust Betrayed?

A personal journey in learning to trust and be trustworthy

When I write about trust betrayed, when I talk about solidarity undermined, it's much more than just what's impacted me. I'm talking rather about patterns of undermining and betrayal that I've experienced among others, things that impact Indigenous people who've been striving to flourish.

I returned to Australia in 1985 following seven years in India and Malaysia. Since then, I've worked alongside Indigenous or Goori families and local communities in contexts ranging from State and Private Schools to community work through Non-Government Organisations (NGOs). In my passion to work for grassroots change in the Logan-Beaudesert region south of Brisbane for example, I supported communities to plan, implement and evaluate processes and structures like:

- Local Justice Initiatives
- Community Justice
- Alternative Governing Structures,

and longer-term projects as on my website www.neilhockey.com.

Over the 28 years I worked alongside families there and throughout the State of Queensland at times, we saw huge gains in a whole lot of areas. We also experienced trust betrayed. There were times when we let each other down badly within our own families and communities. There were times when our trust in government and non-government stakeholders, or in their systems, was broken, or we witnessed heartbreaking moments involving people we strove to support. One example is when I was the state-wide Evaluator for the Queensland Trial Senior Syllabus in Aboriginal and Torres Strait Islander Studies, in 1996-97.

This education initiative in school-community collaboration came out of decades of hard work by Indigenous leaders and their communities across Queensland. It was hard enough to convince many elders that they were welcome in a schooling system that had so often excluded them when they were children. Yet now within that same system they were being invited to share their knowledge of local history, culture and environment. In many of the 15 schools that trialled this initiative across Queensland the processes worked well. This was especially the case due to the persistence and patience of community leaders along with key staff at each school.

However, in a few places when visiting elders began to address student groups, they felt so disrespected and dishonoured that they vowed never to speak again of their knowledge in those situations.

Each community initiative encounters struggles, stories of trust betrayed and rebuilt that are usually best told by the communities themselves, in their time, in their way. As we get to know our neighbours more, we might hear some of those stories. First though, trust must be established.

Contemplate three steps here to gain a broader view of trust.

First, consider some **definitions** of integrity, trust, and love.

Second, learn from **Indigenous perspectives** on the **need for hope** as a basis for integrity, trust and love.

Third, as a transition to chapters 5 and 6, be open to some **Indigenous perspectives** on the **role of truth** as a basis for hope.

Chapter 4: Get Clear on Your Journey: Trust Betrayed?

Define integrity, trust and love

The word **integrity** comes from the Latin word integer, meaning whole or complete. In that sense:

> *Integrity is the inner sense of 'wholeness' deriving from qualities such as honesty and consistency of character.*
>
> **Wikipedia**
>
> *Integrity implies trustworthiness and incorruptibility to a degree that one is incapable of being false to a trust, responsibility or pledge.*
>
> **The Merriam-Webster dictionary**

Now it's clear that we're all capable of betraying a trust or responsibility placed in us. We're all capable of failing to keep a promise. Further, if we're to **regenerate** integrity once we've faltered, we must work at becoming worthy of others' trust once again, becoming trustworthy.

The notion of **trust** is clearly tied to truth and integrity. As a noun, trust is:

> *Assured reliance on the character, ability, strength or truth of someone or something.*
>
> **The Merriam-Webster dictionary**
>
> *Firm belief in the integrity, ability or character of a person or thing; confidence or reliance.*
>
> **The American Heritage® Dictionary of the English Language, 5th Edition**

53

As a verb:

> to believe that someone is good and honest and will not harm you, or that something is safe and reliable.
>
> **Cambridge dictionary**

What is love?

Australians inherit a **fascinating blend of cultural traditions**. In defining love I'll focus on three main ones:

- ✓ Greek (our Western education systems are saturated with Greek thinking)
- ✓ Hebrew/Biblical (is this the "air we breathe" in the West at least?)
- ✓ Goori or Indigenous.

First, the **Greeks** recognised **love's complications and complexities**. Philosophers like Plato and Aristotle talked about 8 different words for it:

1. *Eros* is physical love or sexual desire, involving passion, lust, and/or romance.
2. *Philia* is affectionate love, involving friendship.
3. *Agape* is often defined as unconditional, sacrificial love, as in the love of Jesus the Christ for humanity.
4. *Storge* is the natural love that family members have for one another.
5. *Mania* is excessive love that reaches the point of obsession or madness.

6. *Ludus* is playful, noncommittal love, including things like flirting, seduction, and casual sex.
7. *Pragma* is practical love, based on duty, obligation or logic. It's a factor in all marriages or alliances, where there's probably more to lose by breaking up than staying together.
8. *Philautia* is self-love, like how a person views themselves and how they feel about their own body and mind. But beware, good self-esteem can lead to egomaniacal narcissism!

Second, for the German theologian and philosopher Rudolf Otto, the **Bible's Old and New Testaments** were the main source for what he called the *numinous* (full of divine power). He says in his famous book *The Idea of the Holy*, that this mysterious numinous simultaneously terrifies and fascinates. It's also present in all other religions.

For Otto, the most essential part of salvation history is making rational sense of **the *numinous***:

> ➤ the *tremendous* or terrifying is infused with ideas of **justice and moral will**
> ➤ the *fascinating* is infused with **goodness, mercy and love**, while
> ➤ the *mysterious* is infused with **all moral attributes** in their absolute.

Wow! If only all of us who practise faith were able to live out this combination of divine characteristics. Communities might then be guarded from fanaticism, mere mysticality, and pure rationalism.

Now that's a Good Idea! It's like a symphony, a synchronised vision of the Holy, where **love, goodness, and mercy** are set in a context of the **Terrifying Mystery**.

Third, I paraphrase a bit of what **Professor Japanangka Errol West** wrote in his PhD thesis:

- To live well, we must **constantly regenerate** and **rejuvenate our integrity** as individuals and groups.
- Along the way, we would just naturally **weave together 8 dimensions** – *cultural; spiritual; secular (bureaucratic); intellectual; political; practical; personal;* and *public*.
  (Does that look a bit like THE SPECS?)
- However, **to live with integrity**, to weave together these dimensions doesn't really come naturally, or easily, especially when we get separated from country.
- It takes **daily effort to think deeply** and **practice a balance** of "**spirituality, love, authority** and **compliance**".

Now Japanangka's perspective might come as a bit of a shock. Here, to love fully (as mature adults) takes great effort, deep and complex thinking and compliance with authority, provided the authority has integrity! In his writings he also emphasises the **key role of spirit** in a **marriage with hope and ethics**, to maintain that balance between love, authority and compliance.

That keeps us thinking. To sustain that balance we must keep **cultivating our hopes** in pursuing truth as families, teams, communities and nations.

Discern truth as a basis for hope through facing realities

What might it mean to be fully human through spirit and hope?

What are the connections between who we are, what we know and what we do?

Some **Indigenous educators** insist that to be fully human is:

- to determine one's own life in spiritual harmony with the totality of one's existence
- to confront extreme levels of poverty and
- to sustain both personal and social humanity while
- engaging real oppressions and
- alleviating the relentless grief, stress and discontent which can tend to permeate their lives.

It's only in doing these things they say that we will **understand, explain** and **resolve current crises**.

Think about problems or crises for some in your own city or region where there's often a lack of:

- appropriate housing
- meaningful education for everyone
- adequate standards of health and of appropriate remedies for ill health
- healing from multigenerational legacies of trauma
- hope to live healthy lives or even to survive beyond 50-60 years of age.

These problems tend to be greatest for many Indigenous families. Dealing with immediate needs in each of these areas can be the easiest part. It's not so easy to address the causes.

It's far from being just a "Western" problem. Anyone spending time in non-Western countries would recognise that national and regional leaders in those countries too, tend to negate and deny these same rights to their own Indigenous and lower-class populations. Whether West or East, excluded citizens cry out that to thrive and flourish, everyone must revitalise, strengthen and sustain connections with country (land, seas, and air) as places imbued with spiritual meaning.

That's an issue of truth. What role then for truth?

Regain control in life – develop insight especially within suffering

Sustained suffering strengthens human fears and diminishes people's ability to live with human dignity. Alleviating that relentless grief and discontent depends on renewing traditions. This in turn depends on an ability to discern criteria for leadership and an appropriate form of leadership.

Think back to my story above: the Trial Syllabus where schools were encouraged to include indigenous content in the curriculum. **Japanangka West** among others claimed that this 'inclusion', the "attempted imparting of Aboriginal cultural knowledge and oral history within the present educational systems" was not working. In his view many non-Indigenous educators thought they had a mortgage on educational processes. He describes "three universal human standards" being held to ransom:

1. truth regarding history
2. truth of guilt over Anglo-European education systems' refusal to allow "Aboriginal adjudication" of "White history and behaviour"; and
3. disenfranchisement in relation to their own oral history and cultural knowledge.

Chapter 4: Get Clear on Your Journey: Trust Betrayed?

Richard Trudgen explains how Yolŋu (people) see ways forward out of the crises: dialogue must follow learning processes within both their culture and the dominant culture. Yolŋu ask a key question of any subject:

> "**What is the true, bottom or foundational story** for this particular subject?"

This could be seen as a search for "**the objective truth**" so that new knowledge does not conflict with what Yolŋu see as good solid evidence and **culturally accepted truths** that fit logically with their worldview. However, to be sustainable, 'revitalisation of potential' depends on:

- dealing with primary and "real underlying causes" and
- learning from successes.

Such learning produces cultural practices strengthening students' sense of **identity, place** and **hope**. Clan leaders are central here, as keepers of the *Maḏayin* way (Law) working in partnership with dominant culture teachers in linguistic research.

Japanangka West has a similar vision which **can apply anywhere in the world**. In communities where the dominant language (often, English) is not so well spoken, education's way forward includes:

1. **recognising** management's complex infrastructure and how the system fits together
2. **addressing** barriers to more faithfully translating from an oral- to a writing-based culture
3. **transmitting** uplifting, informative and socially responsive data through sound knowledge systems

4. **ensuring** that the truth, morality and status of the information so transmitted is not recast or diminished in any way
5. **sustaining** negotiations and partnerships with Aboriginal people
6. **confronting** any issues of guilt
7. **underpinning** negotiations with truth, and
8. **achieving** equity

These Indigenous communities' perspectives **help us to discern how** trust and love are birthed by hope, while hope itself is triggered and fed by truth.

> For further reading check the relevant links for **Chapter 4** in the **Recommended Reading List**.

Chapter 4: Get Clear on Your Journey: Trust Betrayed?

Suggestions for Action now

First, think over what you've read about integrity, trust, love, and hope.

As in Part 1, meet again with your small group. Rate (from 1-10) your progress in …

1. Living with integrity personally and as members of various groups.

2. Trusting yourself, others, and being trustworthy.

3. Keeping a healthy balance in the ways you love, as you work on loving unconditionally.

4. Remaining hopeful no matter what is happening to you and around you.

Write down what might be helping or hindering your growth in integrity, trust, love and hope over the past year.

Second, reflect on the **Indigenous perspectives** on trust, love and hope.

Share within your group what you've each learned from reading these Indigenous quotes and descriptions.

In what ways do these perspectives apply among families and communities you know whether Indigenous or not?

Discuss, then plan informal ways of talking through these insights with a wider group.

Third, if you're familiar with education systems where you live and work, respond to the following in your group:

Japanangka West gave reasons why he thought that including Indigenous cultural knowledge in school curricula wasn't working. If you're familiar with this situation in education, discuss how you'd respond to his reasons.

He also gave a list of 8 steps to be included in the way forward for communities where the dominant language (English) is not so well spoken. Which of these steps do you think might be relevant in **every** school context?

Similarly, in what ways do you think that **Richard Trudgen's** Yolŋu ways forward out of social and educational crises might be relevant to society in general?

The essence of this chapter can be said in two words: Truth matters.

Chapter 5 takes a closer look at matters of truth, or **T.R.U.T.H.**

CHAPTER 5

Matters of T.R.U.T.H.
– Go Deeper as Hope Spirals

*If I say "No" to someone and they get angry,
it does not mean I should have said "Yes".*

Sarah Jackson

CHAPTER 5
Matters of T.R.U.T.H.
– Go Deeper as Hope Spirals

> *When times are tough*
> *and trust feels dimmed*
> *not every day's the same.*
>
> *Some you will win*
> *some you might lose but*
> *resist the urge to blame.*
>
> *Then hope –*
> *Rising, deepening in spirals*
> *as truth unfolds*
> *our trembling hearts entwined.*
>
> **Neil Hockey**

While collective or group integrity is a key to **sustaining hope together**, it will always be a life-long struggle to appropriately love our own bodies, hearts and minds.

Prioritise collective *and* personal integrity

I've not been good at keeping boundaries many times. I've not been honest with myself, with others and with my God. My actions haven't always been consistent with my words. At those times I've lacked integrity, partly because I tend to focus on what's happening with others.

So yes, it's a life-long struggle to set boundaries. Keep them but don't lose trust and build walls, for our capacity to trust others is often reduced

Chapter 5: Matters of T.R.U.T.H. – Go Deeper as Hope Spirals

when we feel abandoned, betrayed, abused, even just challenged or contradicted. We might struggle in turn to be faithful to others whether within our families, amongst work colleagues or social friends. A spiral downward might continue from there as others experience us as less trustworthy than we want to be.

Yet it doesn't have to be that way. To spark hope in our minds and hearts, to begin reversing that negative spiral, we must come to realise unfolding layers of truth about ourselves, our histories, our social and cultural environments.

We now live in a world of "post-truth" however. So, our journey in regenerating integrity must be grounded in truth, consistently defined, explained and applied.

Explain truth in practice – but how?

If we are to live
with **common hope** and **purpose**
as families, communities, various teams,
and nations,
how might we **explain truth in practice**?

My goal is to build with you by illustrating from my own journey gently yet provocatively, by:

1. recounting a coronation speech proclaiming colonial truth
2. expanding 5 key aspects of enacting truth to deepen hope
3. pitting some popular (and not-so) theories of truth against postmodern roots of post-truth.

2023 was a year dominated by both controversy and celebration in Australia. The catchcry for those advocating a recognised Voice to

Parliament for Indigenous people was "Voice, Treaty, Truth". In the meantime, while the lobbying, debates, arguments, and divisions over this national referendum were heating up there was a new king crowned.

We've seen in Chapter 4 some Indigenous people groups' passionate resolve to strive for integrity while experiencing colonial justice. British justice is one fountain of global colonial rule. Setting the scene then for Chapters 5 and 6, consider the coronation speech by Britain's PM in 2023. It proclaimed Biblical and political truths that the monarchy says are its core strengths. These confronting colonial truths prompted very mixed reactions in Australia at least, especially from some Indigenous leaders.

Representatives from a host of nations and many religions personally witnessed another challenge to cultivate hope. Hindu Prime Minister Sunak read from the Bible's Colossians Chapter 1. There he would have seen implications of incredible trust/faith and love that spring from a hope inspired by the Good News truth about Jesus the Christ, for he then proclaimed in his reading:

(a) powerful reasons for praying for one another
(b) our potential for patiently persevering in every situation, through
(c) giving thanks joyfully to the Father, for bringing us from darkness to light through His dear Son.

He read that this Son is supreme over all creation, over all physical and spiritual powers and authorities.

Chapter 5: Matters of T.R.U.T.H. – Go Deeper as Hope Spirals

> Then because of this supreme place of Christ in the whole cosmos,
> another reader **challenged the new King**
> (and **presumably, all listeners**)
> to follow the example of Christ in his passion
> to maintain integrity in fulfilling what He was anointed to do
> on earth.

Now that's some challenge, for it's obvious that all kings, leaders, and indeed all families are not always consistent in the way we've been and done what we should be and do.

What then should we do **now**? The PM was full of hope …

"The Coronation … will be a moment of extraordinary national pride.

Together with friends from across the Commonwealth and beyond, we will celebrate the enduring nature of our great monarchy: its constancy, devotion to duty, and service to others.

… (This is) a proud expression of our history, culture, and traditions.

A vivid demonstration of the modern character of our country.

…

In the Abbey where monarchs have been crowned for almost a thousand years, representatives of every faith will play a central role for the first time.

…

So, let's celebrate this weekend with pride in who we are and what we stand for, …

Let's look to the future with hope and optimism."

PM Rishi Sunak

I chose this proclaimed message of hope because it was so widely anticipated and watched across the globe. It also suitably anticipates the message of my book:

> To achieve sustainable change in our lives and situations we must strengthen hope.

Deepen your spiral of hope through T.R.U.T.H.

Hope that lasts springs from being very clear about truth and why it matters. This demands that we ask open-ended or strategic questions such as:

- What first-hand data do we have, including people's lived experiences?
- How can this data be explained?
- What are some reasons or causes for what's been observed, even over decades or centuries?

Identifying and critiquing causes can raise our hopes for change. My acronym TRUTH reinforces this by spelling out 5 key aspects of living out truth. They form a deepening spiral of hope.

As one sentence, it reads:

Truth as
Reality
Unlocks, **U**nearths and **U**ncovers
Trembling, **T**entative and **T**otal
Hearts and **H**opes.

T – Truth, in relation to any person or entity, must mean "true <u>to</u> itself, true <u>for</u> itself, true <u>in</u> and <u>of</u> itself, and true (for a group) for <u>each other</u>

Chapter 5: Matters of T.R.U.T.H. – Go Deeper as Hope Spirals

and <u>their contexts</u>". We need to use this principle to test ourselves and whatever else concerns us.

R – as Reality. Contrary to what many would have us believe, reality is far more than what we "socially construct".

> Think of fruit falling from a tree. Newton did, or so it's said! We might **observe** an apple falling. That's called **empirical** reality.
>
> But there are many other apples that fall, **completely unnoticed** by any observer. This is **actual** reality. It includes the empirical.
>
> Then there's the **unseen gravitational force** causing the event. **Total reality includes** the actual, the empirical, and the unseen that **undergirds them**.

U – Unlocks/Unearths/Uncovers

> When fully considered, apprehended and grasped, truth lays bare what is hidden. Gravitational and magnetic forces are examples from **natural science**.
>
> Can you think of examples from the **social sciences**, such as the kinds of "social glue" realities that keep families, groups, schools, hospitals, or societies running smoothly? Such "glues" are hard to measure, but we certainly feel the effects when they start to come unstuck!

T Trembling/Tentative/Total

> Truth can be a very touchy subject. We're never quite certain. We're tentative, and we often tremble inside as we think about possible consequences. How can we continue to move from feeling

very touchy about it so that we're not just touching the truth but totally embracing it, no matter what it costs us personally? There's potential to transform every aspect of our lives.

H – Hearts/Hopes

Your heart is much more than just a physical organ. The word also describes the core of your mind, will, and emotions.

> *Above all else, guard your heart, for it is the wellspring of life.*
> **Proverbs 4:23**

Do we want to strengthen our hopes?

Our minds, wills and emotions will be challenged and renewed.

This will take open heart surgery.

We urgently need to get down to the truth of the matter.

> *If you wish to become a philosopher, the first thing to realise is that most people go through life with a whole world of beliefs that have no sort of rational justification, and that one man's world of beliefs is apt to be incompatible with another man's, so that they cannot both be right. People's opinions are mainly designed to make them feel comfortable; truth, for most people is a secondary consideration.*
> **Bertrand Russell (1872-1970)**

Chapter 5: Matters of T.R.U.T.H. – Go Deeper as Hope Spirals

Pilate asked, "**What is truth**?" There's no record of anyone answering him. But Jesus had already done so in proclaiming himself as the Way, Truth and Life.

What then is truth? I speak and write here of truth matters or matters of truth. How are we to understand it?

Against post-truth? Get back to basic structures!

What does it mean to **get to the truth** of a matter (whether physical or social)?

What are **explanations for truth** about … (name anything in our chaotic times)?

How can we get to see a little more clearly through 21st century mists of uncertainty and confusion to the heart of the matter of truth?

As just one illustration of how we've arrived at this "post-truth era", the philosopher Roy Bhaskar claimed that postmodernism contributed significantly to the alienation and fragmentation of being, in a world that is increasingly interconnected. According to Britannica and similar sources, postmodernists proclaim:

- there are no **aspects of reality** that are objective
- there are no **statements about reality** that are objectively true or false
- it is not **possible to have knowledge** of such statements (objective knowledge)
- it is impossible for human beings to know some things **with certainty**; and
- there are no objective or absolute **moral values**.

Postmodernists say that reality, knowledge, and value do not derive from objective truth. Rather, they are constructed through **human discourses**, the systems of **thought, knowledge** or **communication** that influence our experience of the world. Any social or political group that controls discourse thus has a lot of power.

Postmodernists claim that consequently:

- ✓ since the established discourses of the 18th century Enlightenment are arbitrary and unjustified, they *can be changed*; and
- ✓ because they reflect the interests and values of the powerful, they *should* be changed
- ✓ they (postmodernists) are **uniquely inclusive** and **democratic**, because their theoretical position allows them to recognise the unjust way the Enlightenment discourses dominated the equally valid perspectives of non-elite groups.

In the 1980s and '90s, various ethnic, cultural, racial and religious groups became the focus of academic advocates. Postmodern critiques of contemporary Western society became the unofficial philosophy of the new movement of identity politics. For better and worse, this has contributed to current debates and conflicts, a whole range of contemporary struggles including the global Black Lives Movement and the 2023 Australian referendum on the Voice to Parliament.

It can be argued that postmodernist influences on thinking and behaviour have contributed to virtually every contemporary national and global crisis – and responses to them – including the way populations responded to the whole pandemic scenario. Those topics are too large for this introductory book.

Since postmodernism evolved from the premodern, classical modern and modern eras it's not surprising that by the late 1990s it began to go

Chapter 5: Matters of T.R.U.T.H. – Go Deeper as Hope Spirals

out of fashion itself. Our current era has slowly become known as post-postmodernism. Wikipedia describes our era as one where "faith, trust, dialogue, performance, and sincerity" are going beyond postmodern irony such as claims like, it's true "there is no such thing as truth".

How then might alternative views of reality be put forward and discussed? The most workable theory of truth is one that best explains causes as basic structures. I'll summarise here what the Dictionary of Critical Realism outlines as six major theories of truth. It's critical we understand this since many people seem to talk past each other in daily conversations and private/public debates, often because they're operating subconsciously from different understandings or theories of the nature of truth.

1. Correspondence theory – We claim "It is raining outside" when it appears so to us. (But we might be on a movie set.)
2. Coherence theory – We claim something to be true because it fits with other beliefs of ours.
3. Consensus theories – We claim something to be true because another person or group also claims it to be true.
4. Idealised consensus theories – We claim something to be true because under specified idealised conditions, others would claim it to be so.
5. Pragmatic theory – We claim something to be true because it appears useful to do so, it suits our purposes.
6. Deflationary theory – There's no point claiming for example that "water is wet". It's just obvious.

How applicable are these theories? We need one that will strengthen and deepen a spiral of hope. I've found "alethic truth" helpful. The Greek word *Aletheia* literally means "the undoing of oblivion, of forgetfulness or forgetting". Alethic truths then are the real or dialectical reasons, grounds or causes of things. They are that which explains them, their objective truth. They are that which captures their essential structure, as when Yolŋu ask:

> "**What is the true, bottom** or **foundational story** for this particular subject?"

Consider the alethic truth of water as basic chemistry for example. Water's essential structure is two hydrogen atoms with one oxygen atom arranged in a certain way. This helps explain how it interacts with other molecules and atoms.

What about social, cultural, and political scenarios however, where discourses for example hold a lot of power to cause certain outcomes? My book provides a framework for working on these scenarios in future books.

Meanwhile email me at hello@transformingtraumatogether.com to extend a conversation personally or with your group, team or organisation.

Chapter 5: Matters of T.R.U.T.H. – Go Deeper as Hope Spirals

Chapter Summary

- The British PM's 2023 coronation speech proclaimed **Biblical** and **political** truths that the monarchy says are its core strengths, the **basis for its integrity**.
- Many welcomed this speech and the whole coronation process. Yet it was confronting for those for whom "**colonial justice**" was a brutal experience.
- A way forward together is to think, live and speak **Truth** as **Reality** with potential to totally **Unlock, Unearth** and **Uncover Tentative, Trembling Hearts** and **Hopes**.
- Late in the 20th century **postmodernism** helped expose the power of **discourses**, systems of **thought, knowledge** and **communication**.
- However, by rejecting objective truth, postmodernist discourse itself tends to **undermine the very fabric** of faith, trust, dialogue, performance and sincerity.
- In our post-postmodernist, **post-truth era**, we need theories of truth that are workable in the real world to **deepen our spiral of hope** and **regenerate integrity**.
- The most workable theory of truth is one that **best explains** reasons, causes or grounds as **basic structures**.

For further reading check the relevant links for **Chapter 5** in the **Recommended Reading List**.

Suggestions for Action now

First, with your group discuss and write down whatever thoughts and feelings you had when seeing, hearing, or reading the PM's bible reading and speech.

What impact (if any) did the coronation event, and the Voice Referendum have on your hopes for the future?

Second, in what ways does my T.R.U.T.H. acronym strengthen or challenge your thinking about truth and reality?

> **Hint**: "Truth" is most often debated using Greek ways of reasoning. Think instead (or research) using other languages, such as various Chinese, Indian, Indigenous, Hebrew, etc. You'll be surprised!

Write down your reflections and share with your group what you're each learning.

Third, as a transition to Chapter 6, write down and discuss examples where you've seen postmodernist influences on identity and integrity within your family, group or society.

What steps might you take to live out more, what you believe to be thinking, doing and speaking truth?

Share and discuss with your group.

CHAPTER 6
Regenerate Identity and Integrity Through Truth

"Hey algorithm
Connect me with people who are able to hold nuance,
who understand that life is always full of paradox,
who weep at violence no matter the optics,
who move slowly enough to let context inform their choices,
who don't try to make things unnecessarily complex
to avoid an uncomfortable truth,
who also don't make things implausibly simple
to fit a narrative.
Connect me with people who are willing to feel
the grief of centuries,
and are still, somehow, able to love the world."

A post circulating on fb in October 2023 by
abigail.rose.clarke

CHAPTER 6
Regenerate Identity and Integrity Through Truth

The **challenge from Chapter 5** was:

> If we are to live
> with common hope and purpose
> as families, communities, various teams and nations,
> how might we explain truth in practice?

Our post-truth journeys can be long and difficult. Engaging truth though enables us to restore, regenerate and consolidate identity and integrity over a lifetime. All previous eras had their own narratives, storylines and life cycles. Post-truth is now threaded through our times: pandemics, current warzones, climate change, wokeism, religious freedoms and beliefs, Australia's referendum, 2024 political elections etc.

Passions associated with each issue or cause rise or fall with social, economic and political changes. Emerging narratives and counter-narratives interact, compete, adapt, develop and die. We're all caught up in this swirling stream. Negotiating our journeys through potential minefields presents huge challenges! It might involve many years of dismantling or deconstructing fictional elements in our pasts. There are usually fearful futures to confront and conquer along the way.

> To lead with hope, we need solid grounds
> in the disorder of a post-truth era
> of emerging mass-psychoses.

Chapter 6: Regenerate Identity and Integrity Through Truth

Distinguish lawful from legal: an aid in navigating post-truth

One example of how we might counteract the way post-truth stories develop and dominate is to distinguish between lawful and legal. These apparently similar terms have competed over the past two centuries. The implications are profound despite it seeming like a small distinction. A quote from the site grammarhow clarifies the point:

> *Legal can sometimes encompass actions permissible under the law but not necessarily ethical. For instance, certain business practices might be legal but not universally considered moral. Lawful suggests a more holistic compliance with the spirit and ethics of the law, often implying a moral judgment.*
>
> **grammarhow**

According to data compiled using the Google Ngram Viewer the word "Legal" is now used significantly more than the word "Lawful". There's no record of where or how this data was collected. It's relevant though to current crises in Australia such as domestic violence, crime rates, even debate around pandemics and responses to them, whether by governments or populations in general. Early in the 1800s the gap between usage of "Legal" and "Lawful" was very small. By 2019 "Legal" was over 20 times more common than "Lawful". My experience working with young people and their families in the criminal justice system backs this up.

Truth is being questioned in the Dock – an Indigenous perspective

This chapter explores consequences across all societies but particularly Indigenous peoples, where so much evidence points to them being massively over-represented in the criminal justice system. Some historical reasons for this lie in Indigenous law systems compared to Indigenous knowledge and experience of western law.

According to Richard Trudgen's account the main challenge to Arnhem Land's Yolŋu Law or *Madayin* began with fifty years of wars. This was followed by enforced missions, the 1980s nightmare of 'self-determination' and the ongoing living hell of welfare dependency, an institutionalised violence wrapped up in subtle, ethnocentric paternalism.

The past four years have been harder than ever. A journey typical of Indigenous communities worldwide is shared below by Yolŋu. It illuminates stress and suffering endured by many struggling to maintain integrity. Written 10 May 2023 on the "Why Warriors" Facebook page and shared with Richard Trudgen's permission, it helps us all to discern what we might need to do.

> *Many say we need to work for generational change.*
>
> *Well-known author and Arnhem Land Community Educator Richard Trudgen said last week, "Well, the generational change that the present Balanda (white man's) colonial system has delivered to the Yolŋu people of Arnhem Land is*
>
> - *from lawfulness to lawlessness;*
> - *from functioning communities to dysfunctional ones;*
> - *from high levels of employment to massive unemployment;*
> - *from international trade and business development to almost no business development and international trade;*
> - *from very low levels of morbidity and mortality to the highest disease and death rates in the world;*
> - *from low jailing rates to the highest imprisonment rates in the world;*
> - *from a hungry desire for education to almost no appetite for education or training.*

Chapter 6: Regenerate Identity and Integrity Through Truth

How many more disastrous world records in human disempowerment does Australia want to deliver to their First Nations people just because Yolŋu and other traditional Aboriginal people do not speak English well and do not understand British culture?"

In 2005, thirty-eight traditional Yolŋu (Aboriginal) laws were shared with the Australian English-speaking public for the first time in 200 years. These laws came out of the higher combined Dhuwa clan Ngaarra parliaments of northeast Arnhem Land. These are some of the laws that all Yolŋu have assented to through a ceremonial process for thousands of years.

Yolŋu believe these laws were given to them by the Great Creator Spirit Waŋarr, through the Creator Spirits, and they have maintained them through many thousands of years until today.

Some will ask, "So if they have these traditional laws, why is there so much lawlessness"? The lawlessness we see now is a very recent development. Richard continues, "When I came to live with Yolŋu in the 1970s, Yolŋu communities were some of Australia's safest, most peaceful and lawful places, especially for young single women. We never had to lock our homes or worry about being assaulted. And no one would steal anything. The traditional Yolŋu laws kept everyone safe."

These traditional laws have been undermined or broken down today. This is due to the Territory and Federal governments failing to acknowledge the original Australian law operating in Yolŋu and other Aboriginal communities across the NT.

Most of the lawlessness we now see in Aboriginal communities and major centres comes from very confused, angry Aboriginal youth. This is a product of the failed relationship between the traditional First Nations people and the mainstream English-speaking Balanda people.

Why Warriors Pty Ltd

These issues raised by Why Warriors are simple yet highly complex, as illustrated in the highly readable "*Why Warriors Lie Down and Die*". It's one of the best Australian books on cross-cultural community development. Issues across Australia vary with many factors so if you're keen to follow up the points mentioned, engage with appropriate Indigenous people where you are.

My own life-long passion and this chapter's focus remain on needs within traumatised communities globally. These 21st century issues have long been relevant to most Indigenous communities everywhere. The 2023 coronation of King Charles simply brought a lot of memories to the surface in Australia at least.

Reflect on a king's coronation in history – deeply challenging national integrity?

That's how journalist Stan Grant and others saw it. Invited to contribute to the ABC's coverage as part of a discussion about the monarchy's legacy, he pointed out that:

- **the crown represents** the invasion and theft of his people's land
- **in the name of the crown** his people were segregated on missions and reserves
- police wearing the **seal of the crown** took children from their families
- **under the crown** his people across the country were massacred
- **under that same crown**, Australian Indigenous people remain the most impoverished and imprisoned people in the country.

Stan Grant spoke with maturity and respect from his community life experience. Yet many vehemently opposed him. Wherever we stand on this spectrum the whole debate tugs at our sense of integrity – as individuals, communities, and as a nation.

Chapter 6: Regenerate Identity and Integrity Through Truth

> *Through my Wiradjuri family I learned Yindyamarra. Yindyamarra is respect. During the coronation coverage I spoke of Yindyamarra for those who support the monarchy even as I confront the darkness of colonisation and empire. I speak truth with love because that is who I am. If I did not offer Yindyamarra, my ancestors would be ashamed of me. They would also be ashamed of me if **I did not speak up for justice**. I speak of truth, not grievance. Yet that is not how it has been reported. (My emphasis)*
>
> **Stan Grant**

Stan's challenge was twofold here: Australia can't continue to live in the fantasy that pretends we have transcended this history; we owe it to ourselves to be better.

> *Truths. Hard truths. Truths not told with hate – truths offered with love. Yes, love. I repeatedly said that these truths are spoken with love for the Australia we have never been.*
>
> *Love that inspired my grandfather – a Wiradjuri man – to fight in World War II for a country that didn't recognise his full humanity, let alone his citizenship. My grandfather who kept by his bed the Bible and the works of Shakespeare. A Wiradjuri man who knew that he had a place in the world.*
>
> **Stan Grant**

As a journalist whose integrity is well known across the world, Stan recounts how he and his family are regularly racially mocked or abused on social media in his own country. As a human like us all, Stan acknowledged that:

> *I am not perfect. But I try to live a good life. I try to be kind. I love my family. I love my people. I love the idea of what our country could be. I am a person of God and I know God is on the side of justice.*
>
> *Sadly, it seems there is no place in the media for love, kindness, goodness or God. There is no place in the media for respect.*
>
> **Stan Grant**

Soon after this mainstream and social media firestorm, Stan stepped down from his duties as a journalist. He expressed dismay at the constant tendency of the media to turn public discussion into an amusement park.

> *I take time out because we have shown again that our history – our hard truth – is too big, too fragile, too precious for the media. The media sees only battle lines, not bridges. It sees only politics.*
>
> **Stan Grant**

How then might we see past the politics, past the perceived legalities, to re-engage a reality of morality? What a challenge!

Engage truth, restore identity, regenerate integrity – grieving's hard roads

This chapter so far has shown a little of the depth of suffering and grief among Indigenous people in Australia, a picture resonating with Indigenous peoples everywhere.

Chapter 6: Regenerate Identity and Integrity Through Truth

As a bridge to Part 3 and Chapter 7 of this book, what might we learn from **Gerry Taiaiake Alfred**, a Canadian Native American professor? Alfred writes regarding the long hard road of recovery from collective grief and trauma. He reflects pleas outlined above by both *Why Warriors* and Stan Grant. His book *"Peace, Power, Righteousness: an indigenous manifesto"* is aimed at revitalising community governance around a specific ritual used for condolence, healing and rebuilding among his people. He says it's a deliberate move away from the revolutionary objectives of the Native movement's earlier phases.

They see this move as imperative to "replace the dividing, alienating and exploitative notions based on fear, that drive politics inside and outside Native communities today". The goal now amongst many groups is to revitalise traditional culture, gaining access to power through:

- ➢ balancing the diverse aspects of their being
- ➢ harmonising with the natural forces that exist outside of them
- ➢ respect for the integrity of others and diverse forms of power, and
- ➢ knowledge of ritual.

Within this ritual, whether relations were between two individuals, families, states, or nations, it was imperative he says, by their Law, to negotiate lasting peace in

> *respectful (co-equal) friendship and alliance, [where] any interference with the other partner's autonomy, freedom or powers was expressly forbidden. So long as these principles were respected, the relationship would be peaceful, harmonious and just.*
>
> **Taiaiake Alfred**

Alfred claims that the condolence ritual's structure, words and deep meaning:

- ✓ express the transformative power inherent in many healing traditions
- ✓ represent a way of bringing people back to the power of reason (a priority over material wealth)
- ✓ are a return to 'traditional' common beliefs, values, and principles, political values to educate their nation's new generation of leaders who will love and sacrifice for their people.

What does all this have to do with those of us who might (so far!) have no contact with Indigenous people? Alfred says clearly that he wrote "Peace, Power, Righteousness" for all the citizens of his country of Canada.

What then about Australian society or wherever you might be? We all struggle with grief. According to psychologists there might be no deeper grief than that of being separated from your roots, the place of your ancestors and birth.

To conclude this chapter then I outline some issues faced by Australian musician, writer and actor Nick Cave. I've chosen Cave because his life story across several cultures mirrors a journey travelled by many Indigenous friends in Australia, India and elsewhere. It's a search for what is Lawful in a modern, postmodern and post-postmodern world heavily divided over categories of the Legal.

Chapter 6: Regenerate Identity and Integrity Through Truth

To **summarise just a few aspects**, based mainly on Wikipedia:

- ➢ Cave's turbulent teenage years were influenced by a wide range of literature, music and educational institutions
- ➢ his music overall seems characterised too by emotional intensity, a wide variety of influences and lyrical obsessions with death, religion, love and violence
- ➢ his father dying suddenly in a car accident created a vacuum in his life at 21
- ➢ grief was later compounded: one son dying at 15, another at 22
- ➢ he tends to spurn grief's medicalised therapeutic language, instead treating death and bereavement not strictly privately, but in culturally collective ways
- ➢ reading the Bible avidly, he's said that any true love song is for God, ascribing his music's mellowing to a shift in focus from Old Testament to New
- ➢ his views on faith, religion, God's reality, politics and culture seem to fluctuate wildly, making fascinating reading as a passionate search for personal and political integrity.

Chapter Summary

1. Distinguishing lawful from legal will help us navigate and counteract post-truth stories developing and dominating.
2. Truth questioned in the Dock – Contrast "truth" in Indigenous experience of western law as "legal", with their own views as moral and ethical.
3. This distinction is a helpful lens for discerning truth in contemporary crises in sectors like health, education, crime and domestic or gender violence.
4. Colonial histories deeply challenge our sense of national integrity.
5. It's neither possible nor helpful to pretend we've transcended these histories.
6. It *is* possible to see past the politics, the perceived legalities, to *re-engage a reality of morality.*
7. Mutual respect for everyone's autonomy, freedom and powers would contribute greatly to communities becoming more peaceful, harmonious and just.
8. The power of wealth can be minimised through 'traditional' common beliefs, values, principles and political values, restoring leaders to sacrificial love.
9. Grieving, death and bereavement are opportunities to collectively regenerate cultural roots of integrity.

For further reading check the relevant links for **Chapter 6** in the **Recommended Reading List**.

Chapter 6: Regenerate Identity and Integrity Through Truth

Suggestions for Action now

First, share in your family, group or team, your experiences of the impact of "post-truth".

> What ways have you found helpful in navigating and counteracting these trends?

Second, discuss with your group your responses to reading the *Why Warriors* account of changes over recent decades.

> How is this account relevant to where you live?

Third, there have been widely different responses to Stan Grant's contribution in covering the coronation.

> How might your group reconcile these different responses?

Fourth, Taiaiake Alfred speaks of revitalising his people's traditional common beliefs, values, principles and political values.

> Discuss within your group, traditions you want to draw upon to help raise up leaders in negating wealth's power in your place.

Fifth, share within your group situations when you've experienced times of grieving, death and bereavement as regenerating integrity with others.

It's one thing to experience special times of regenerating integrity. Sustaining integrity together is the challenge. I take this up now in Part 3.

PART 3
Sustain Collective Integrity: Make Change a Habit!

Have you, your friends or colleagues recently made good progress towards your goals? You might even have established a good level of friendship, stability, collaboration or teamwork over several years. Then suddenly the unexpected happens. Old habits and forgotten patterns of behaviour begin to re-emerge, or there's a sudden eruption of thoughts and difficult emotions when you thought all that had been dealt with long ago.

What caused this volcanic surge now? Why such strong emotions?

Can you trust yourselves and your judgments with the same level of confidence?

It's easier to sustain change long-term once you regain those healthy patterns. My challenge here is: prepare more ground for your persistent hard work! What seems lost must be regained!

From my experience we can learn much by immersing ourselves in situations quite different from our own day-to-day cultural ways of life. Part 3 builds on previous sections. I extend and deepen my personal stories across the years in India and Malaysia, inviting each reader:

- ➢ absorb yourself in each of my stories
- ➢ creatively think through and apply what comes to mind to your own situation
- ➢ share your reflections with a small group of others in your network.

Chapter 7 explores how living by truth with renewed hope sustains our capacity to love unconditionally, overcoming overwhelming obstacles as trust is restored over time.

Chapter 8 shows how truth really matters at all levels across every action by people persevering in developing six essential qualities. It's a journey in confronting fears through love, refreshing your whole way of life.

Chapter 9 spells out the need for thinking and working at deeper levels. It outlines key elements of putting truth into practice. These disciplines will give you a strong foundation for facing life's daily realities and responsibilities. Working together, they strengthen every aspect of our life-long journey in a spiral leading from self-esteem to total well-being, even amid suffering as trauma is being transformed.

CHAPTER 7

Restore Trust, Pursue Truth

"Hope is not a lottery ticket you can sit on the sofa and clutch, feeling lucky. It is an axe you break down doors with, in an emergency. Hope should shove you out the door, because it will take everything you have to steer the future away from endless war, from the annihilation of the earth's treasures and the grinding down of the poor and marginal ... To hope is to give yourself to the future – and that commitment to the future is what makes the present inhabitable."

Rebecca Solnit

CHAPTER 7
Restore Trust, Pursue Truth

There are ups and downs in learning to restore trust. My part in stories from India began in the late '70s. I reflect on times in three places most meaningful to me:

- ➢ early years in **Delhi** with many seeking truth
- ➢ connections with **north-eastern States**, striving to live out truth
- ➢ an "insignificant" town in **central India**, a commitment to truth, love and justice.

> To be transformative, trust must be nurtured over years.
> It's in trusting others and being trusted
> that our collective capacity to act further on truth
> is enhanced and sustained.

A personal journey in consolidating trust for sustainable integrity

At the age of fifteen I started mingling with troubled young people across inner-city Brisbane and its North-side suburbs. It was a small beginning. Building mutual trust with those who felt their trust had been betrayed then led to my working in other parts of Australia, India, and Malaysia.

Looking back, that's when I began to grapple with my six key TRAUMA actions, goals to strive for, and ways to get there. Then amid the craziness of my teens through twenties I started to appreciate more of life's lessons reflected in the 4 "R" assumptions and the 6 principles of trauma-informed care and practice (see Chapter 3).

Chapter 7: Restore Trust, Pursue Truth

A short version of growth in our community work since the late 70s illustrates this, building a residential therapeutic community with Indian friends in New Delhi. We called it *Aashiana*, meaning nest, beautiful home or dwelling place. It later became *Sahara House*, meaning rest, shelter or refuge.

After seven years all non-Indians in our community left due to visa issues. Everyone else continued. By the early 90s *Sahara House* became a leading model for working with intravenous drug users across the country. Sister projects were established in six other cities: Shillong, Kohima, Imphal (all in north-eastern States), Mumbai, Pune and Hyderabad.

From the beginning there were criteria for entry into our Delhi community. These included:

- acknowledge your personal need in a fractured world
- commit to collectively pursue truth and
- act on that truth within a context of unconditional yet confronting love.

We simply, but with considerable anguish and at times amid hurtful conflict, shared our lives with whoever came along: Indians from all parts of the country, Afghan, African, Iranian, and Malaysian students, each speaking their own language but with English in common. From time to time there was of course the odd Aussie, Pom, Yank or Kiwi.

There were Hindus of all persuasions, along with Muslims, Buddhists, Zoroastrians, Dalits, Jews and Christians of whatever sort you could imagine. Almost daily we studied key figures within all these major or minor Indian cultural and religious traditions from throughout Indian history, debating their teachings and life's work. All this took place while working daily with the local poor wherever they were. We learnt that transformative trust must be nurtured over years as time permits by acting on truth as we currently grasp it, sustained by hope of change.

Acknowledge your hope fluctuating over time

Confronted by truth, how might you imagine hope in action?

This active, bursting-out-everywhere hope fronted up to our pleasantly chaotic *Aashiana* environment on Maundy Thursday, 1980. Known as "Chinky" throughout Delhi and other north Indian cities he had some serious addictive habits and was desperate to break them. After an equally serious questioning process Chinky was admitted to the community. He lasted 6 months with us. His cravings took over and he made the choice to leave. On Maundy Thursday 1982 Chinky turned up again on our doorstep begging to be re-admitted, which he was on certain strict conditions.

I still have notes of my reflections while sleeping on the floor in shifts alongside his bed at the Safdarjang Hospital while he went through cold turkey. However again although recovering well he was back on the streets within another six months. This was heart-wrenching for everyone. He was a delightful fun-loving presence. Everyone came to know his favourite worship songs and his passion for serving alongside the poor was clear.

Many more months passed. Just before Maundy Thursday 1984 we heard that Chinky had died alone during the night on the streets in Delhi's Connaught Place. This tragedy is forever in my memory as a reminder that Maundy Thursday or Passover is a time of decision amongst broad and complex issues around addictions of many kinds. It's a time to choose between life or death, to embrace deliverance and commit to that journey or reject resurrection life, that power of the Spirit who raised Jesus from the dead.

Chapter 7: Restore Trust, Pursue Truth

There's a chain then, a circle, or better still a deepening spiral as life moves through us: Truth → Hope → Love and Trust → Growth in Integrity

We all act on what we see or believe to be true whether consciously or not. How painful is the challenge though when we're confronted with conflicting views on the truth of a matter.

Learn from trauma in tribal north-east India

On this book's front cover, I'm wearing a jacket and shoulder bag. These are gifts from Manipuri Tangkhul friends in northeast India. I've had links with them and others from surrounding states since 1978. To me the gifts symbolise a commitment to truth, justice and peace amongst all the groups of that region.

> There is outrage in India ...
> opposing groups (with vested interests)
> acting on what they believe and feel strongly
> to be true

In mid-2023 there were riots in Manipur, not for the first time. The conflicts have highly complex roots going back generations. Their trauma challenges us to work through the roots of our own personal and national traumas with dignity and hope. Headlines of that time eventually reported "Outrage in India". People across the country were asking once again, "How can this be true of us as a nation of communities?"

A video had belatedly emerged of two Manipuri tribal women being paraded naked, subjected to blatant acts of sexual assault by a mob of men. Relatives of the women filed a police complaint alleging that one of the women was subsequently gangraped and killed. The survivor told reporters that another woman in her 50s was also allegedly stripped, while the father and brother of a 21-year-old woman were killed.

Various media sources reported since then that the state had been effectively torn in two:

- both communities attacked each other's residences and vehicles
- some churches and temples were burnt down
- more than 140 people were killed
- over 60,000 were displaced as refugees to surrounding States.

The Indian Prime Minister Modi sought to assure the nation that "the law will take its course with all its might. What happened with the daughters of Manipur can never be forgiven". In July 2023 an editorial in the Aljazeera media asked, "Can Manipur ever trust India again?"

According to **this editorial**:

- ➢ it's a humanitarian crisis, a civil war where women's bodies have been used as instruments of coercion and subjugation
- ➢ the match had been lit long ago via political decisions by the British, then local and national Indian leaders
- ➢ the flame was kept alive by military and sexual politics alienating generations of Manipuris and now tearing the state apart
- ➢ in some ways Manipur's plight is mirrored throughout India where in state after state police are being used as the ruling party's police instead of protecting its citizens' lives and property, a direct legacy of India's 1861 colonial Police Act
- ➢ generations of people from the northeast have been victims of unbridled racism – including physical violence and sexualisation
- ➢ the region's challenges and cries for help are routinely ignored in the corridors of power and media channels
- ➢ this then is the current situation: those who suffer must learn to wipe their own tears, pick up the pieces, start life afresh, stop looking outside for assistance.

Chapter 7: Restore Trust, Pursue Truth

The writer then poses two questions:

1. Why blame the people of the northeast if they feel betrayed?
2. Why blame them if they're always looking back at the Instruments of Accession they signed more than seven decades ago amid hope and expectations?

That editor concludes "The Indian State has failed them. Yet again".

How might we use this tragedy to deepen our own spirals of hope, especially regarding relations with governments wherever we are?

Celebrate your own Nagod – an "insignificant" town in central India

In the early 1980s India's social and political climate was somewhat like now. A few couples, university graduates who'd been part of *Aashiana* chose to use their knowledge and skills to work with semi-rural communities in Central India. One couple stayed on. Their story follows, adapted from their website.

> (W)hat they (the local people) need is a quality pathway forward upon which they can exercise their skills and voices. The talent is here; all it needs is proper cultivation and encouragement, and to be taken seriously.
>
> **Our History**
> Satya Niketan (House of Truth) Higher Secondary School has been serving Nagod and the surrounding villages since 1985 shortly after Chandrakant and Rebecca Shourie moved to town. Their academic backgrounds were rooted in some of India's great universities. They wanted to bring that level of academic quality to Nagod.

> The school started with just a handful of students. In recent years we've grown to upwards of one thousand students. Swati and Ashish, two of the Shourie's children, have stayed in Nagod to help run the school well into the future. It is our great pleasure to serve the Nagod community as best as we are able.
>
> **Our Vision**
> To raise up a generation of young people unhindered by the constraints of poverty, empowered to produce meaningful change in their communities, inspired to live in hope, and committed to the flourishing of their nation and the world.
>
> The school's slogan is "To the Victory of: Truth – Love – Justice".
>
> **Our Leadership**
> As founders and leaders of this institution we take great care and pride in doing our best for our staff and our students. We are constantly meeting together to discuss and implement ways to keep our institution relevant and impactful according to the changing needs and standards that we face in today's fast-paced world.

Our modern (but ever human) tendency is to criticise communities that lie at society's margins. We need to move from criticising them to celebrating what they have to offer in life. It's up to you and me, all of us who learn about Nagod from a distance, to find out where *we* are called to live and serve. It's an invitation to seek out the "insignificant places" in our own worlds that could do with more truth, love and justice.

This calls for ongoing transformations that will entirely pervade us. This is your focus in Chapter 8.

Chapter 7: Restore Trust, Pursue Truth

Chapter Summary

- ✓ nurture your small beginnings – they can flourish when the time's right
- ✓ it's a fractured world – so acknowledge your personal needs
- ✓ cultivate an environment of unconditional yet confronting love
- ✓ in that environment, commit to pursue truth with those around you
- ✓ live out that truth
- ✓ cultivate a lifestyle of open minds, open hearts, open hands and open homes
- ✓ truth is a spark that keeps our flame of hope burning
- ✓ hope in turn fosters our capacity to trust, to love again and so rebuild integrity
- ✓ we can lose trust not just in people, but in groups, organisations and institutions
- ✓ to endure, hope must be fed by streams of truth intermingled with suffering, even death
- ✓ social conflict exposes women as instruments of coercion and subjugation
- ✓ historical political decisions by colonial leaders have major consequences
- ✓ local differences in history and culture are often despised or ignored
- ✓ local cries for help are often ignored in the corridors of power and media channels
- ✓ those who suffer must often start life afresh and stop looking to the State for assistance
- ✓ when we persevere, truth, love and justice eventually bear fruit.

For further reading check the relevant links for **Chapter 7** in the **Recommended Reading List**.

Suggestions for Action now

Take some time to write a response to each of the following:

1. Reading about the growth of Sahara House or Satya Niketan, what similar groups came to your mind either from history or the present?

2. What strikes you most about such groups?

3. List three (or more) lifestyle issues where you want to make changes.

4. What parallels might you see between the experiences of the tribal peoples of India's north-east, and Indigenous people in your own region or country?

5. Discuss your responses with people in your trusted circle of family, friends, or colleagues and encourage each other to take constructive action.

In the next chapter
       I explore more deeply
              connections between truth, love and justice.

CHAPTER 8

Making Truth MATTers Entirely Pervade You

Many people who heard him say these things
trusted in him.
So, Jesus said to the Judeans who had trusted in him,
"If you obey my words,
if you continue in my teachings,
then you really are my disciples,
you will know the truth
and the truth will make you free".

Jesus the Christ (Yeshua ha Mashiach)
John 8: 30-32

CHAPTER 8
Making Truth MATTers Entirely Pervade You

Threaded throughout this chapter are stories of my personal journeys in health and well-being over the past 60 years.

Sustain integrity through life's inevitable rhythms – but how?

> How might we best sustain transformation
> towards collective integrity
> (our hope in action)
> through life's inevitable rhythms
> of success and failure?

I can best summarise this challenge and its resolution here and in the next chapter by using the acronym MATTERS.

To sustain hope over many years your choices and my choices must eventually contain **7 key components** inspired here by the late Roy Bhaskar. Possibly one of the greatest philosophers in our modern era with a brilliant mind, he's described as open, funny, gregarious and enormously generous. That's how I knew him too over twelve years, working a little alongside him. He challenged everyone to keep working out his ideas in practice.

My **first four components** (Chapter 8) deal with a practical vision of transformation that pervades every aspect of our lives. The **final three** (Chapter 9) comprise a web that mutually supports and sustains that

Chapter 8: Making Truth MATTers Entirely Pervade You

vision. Together they craft our deepening spiral of consolidating trust and integrity. It's a matter of putting truth (and the hope it inspires) into action.

To help me live this out I've put it all together as an acronym –

Truth MATTERS for all:

> M – **Micro, Macro,** and **Meta** levels of our lives
> A – **Across** all habitual **Actions** and inactions, building on our lives as radically
> T – **Transformed, Transformative, Trustworthy** agents within
> T – **Totalising, Transformist** and **Transitional** praxis that mutually strengthens the chain
> E – **Esteem** (self- and mutual-) ←→ **Eudaimonia** (a journey to Total Wellbeing and flourishing), sustained ultimately by our
> R – **Reflexive** (objectively observing our subjective responses)
> S – **Selves**, alone and together

In this chapter I'll spell out what I mean for the M.A.T.T. of the acronym, then look at the E.R.S. components in Chapter 9, where I illustrate my own response to this big challenge to sustain our hope of consolidating collective integrity.

Live life to the full at Micro, Macro, and Meta levels

You've possibly heard the terms micro-economics and macro-economics. You also might have heard of a framework often used in social work research: the levels micro (for individuals), meso (for groups), and macro (for institutions and policies). Here though I'm writing about the micro, macro, and meta levels of our lives in general.

Micro

I've spent much of my life working on the spiritual core of our existence. In this book I'm also looking at the places our spirits dwell, our bodies. The micro level refers to not just our bodies, but each separate organ and the microscopic mitochondria and cells that form each organ. It refers also to how all our bodily systems work together, including our brains, minds, and yes, our spirits as well.

Soon after moving around in my city of Brisbane as a fifteen-year-old I started hearing of ways to improve health other than with medications. That got my attention. I'd been suffering from flu-type infections regularly from the age of ten. I used to be bed-ridden for three weeks at a time every two years This continued until I turned 25. Each time the prescribed treatment was heavy doses of antibiotics.

I started university studies at seventeen and began experimenting with a more vegetarian diet, fasting regularly for both spiritual and physical benefits. After graduating I didn't look after my health while teaching in central Queensland. Only in the late 1990s did I really look closely at why my body started reacting strongly to many pesticides or additives in various foods and drinks. Since then I've been pursuing more truth about how our bodies work. I'm very grateful for this journey.

One big question stands out:

> How might we best **sustain the integrity of our bodies**
> through an **integrated approach** to medical care
> that involves **natural means** (often referred to as complementary medicine)
> along with the **alternatives** that **pharmaceutical** drugs
> or conventional western medicine offer?

This question prompts others in the macro and meta dimensions.

Macro and **Meta**

These prefixes come from Greek. Macro means "large" or "big," while meta means "beyond" or "transcending". I apply them here to well-being, specifically in relation to mental or spiritual.

Macro can then refer to the overall structure or organisation of how small or larger groups, or an entire society, respond to mental health including trauma issues, rather than specific details, contexts or situations. In other words, macro refers here to the **overall perspective** or **view**.

A macro view of my micro-level health issues above must encompass a broad range of responses to remedies in health (e.g. social, political, and economic). This includes an often-blanket approach to treating bacterial infections with antibiotics.

Meta goes beyond (or deeper than) that macro view to analysing and examining in detail all the **underlying factors** that contribute to what's happening. Now since this book explores root causes and consequences of hurt and trauma, this meta-analysis is a form of critique.

> For transformation to be all pervading and sustainable
> it's necessary
> that our critique should do two things

First, it must *identify what is missing* or incomplete in thinking about any context.

Second, it should *explain why* it's missing. This means identifying any social, economic or political (etc.) factors that keep things the way they are, instead of empowering people for lasting transformation.

Develop habitual Actions and in-Actions

We impact each other and our world through both what we do and what we don't do. There are things we're **not doing** that we could benefit by doing. Then there are things we're **doing** that we would benefit by not doing. That's why my 'A' in MATTERS refers to pursuing truth in both our actions and our inactions.

Since I started paying close attention to my lifestyle's impact on my physical body, I've had to change many habits. It's meant stopping doing a lot of things and starting doing many others. Periodically I've been under great pressure with looming deadlines, so retired by 8pm then started the day's work anywhere between 1am and 3am. That can't be continued for long I can guarantee!

People who've lived or worked with me chuckle at my lifestyle, including eating habits which have sometimes seemed strange. It's taken many years to get consistent in turning my day upside down so to speak. I now start working days at sunset after a reasonably good meal then aiming to get a good 8 hours' sleep (physical in-Action) before 4.30am. Rising before or with the birds gives time to prepare a substantial breakfast and do a half hour's exercise before work continues. If the day stretches out, I'll have a light snack during the day before the evening meal. When with other family members or friends though, I'm always happy to adapt.

Another most significant change for me in recent years has been to take a particular full day's rest every week as far as possible.

Become Transformed, Transformative and Trustworthy people – grounded through Totalising, Transformist and Transitional praxis

By crafting our lives around habitual actions and inactions we're strengthened to persevere in commitments to transformation and change. This becomes a lifestyle whereby as people or agents we're more likely

Chapter 8: Making Truth MATTers Entirely Pervade You

to be **Transformed, Transformative** and **Trustworthy**. This is my first T in M.A.T.T.

Transformed agents

Definitions of "transform" talk about:

- a profound change in form, appearance or structure from one stage to the next
- a change in condition, nature or character
- an ongoing process that requires commitment, perseverance, a willingness to change and hard work
- a change using one's own tissue or resources, yet it's not done in isolation

Several dictionary definitions say it suggests an abrupt change, a startling change induced by, or "as if by" magic or a supernatural power.

More fascinating still are insights we get from looking at the word's origins. In Greek it's "metamorphose" combining two words:

1. "meta" meaning change after being with, while
2. "morphoo" means to change form in keeping with an inner reality

So, dictionaries say "metamorphoo" can mean **first** an outward change that reflects an inner reality.

Second, that inner reality can arise from and be nurtured by participating in community with others.

Third, there are many references to those "others" as potentially including any one amongst a range of supernatural powers.

A quote from that ancient Greco/Roman world makes sense here:

> So, I exhort you brothers and sisters, in view of God's mercies, offer yourselves as a sacrifice, not dead, but living and set apart for the living God. This will please him. It's the logical "Temple worship" for you. In other words, don't let this age, the world and its systems squeeze you into its mould. Instead, **continually go on being transformed** by the renewing of your minds …
>
> **Paul the Apostle,** Romans 12:1-2 (my paraphrase)

Sooner or later life teaches us how interdependent we are. We also learn how easily we're impacted by the world's systems. So, to sustain change in our own lives, being continually transformed is not sufficient. We must also maintain a transformative stance towards everything around us.

Transformative agents

We apply this word as an adjective when we talk of a transformative **experience** that had a life-changing impact on us. However, when more decisive and intentional we take up a transformative **stance** by directing our efforts at changing the environment external to ourselves. For example:

- ➢ transformative **arts** use activities like storytelling, music or painting to help individuals or groups grow mentally and emotionally in constructive ways
- ➢ transformative **learning** can be powerful over time for example in mentoring, coaching or job shadowing processes
- ➢ transformative **learning theory** explains how we receive, process and then (hopefully!) apply new information constantly

Chapter 8: Making Truth MATTers Entirely Pervade You

- transformative **educators** bring out the best in learners, developing their faculties and powers, providing the learners feel valued, acknowledged, safe and included
- transformative or transformational **leaders** have integrity, they inspire, support, encourage critical thinking and problem-solving in highly considerate ways
- transformative **justice** is a community based and healing centred response to harm, abuse or injustice without creating more violence or relying on the state

Trustworthy agents

Initially we mightn't think this needs explaining. Take time though to consider whether you and others in your group are:

- ✓ good and upright in character
- ✓ dependable, faithful and loyal, true, able to keep confidences
- ✓ honest in handling money, not able to be corrupted in business dealings

Without these qualities, relationships can quickly become toxic and highly dysfunctional. But all's good so far (imagine)! You and your family, group or team are transformed, transformative and trustworthy in the way you function and work as people. This must ground your work.

Let's look again at **praxis**. Remember praxis is **the process** (according to Wikipedia) by which "a theory, lesson, or skill is **enacted, embodied, realised, applied**, or put into practice". It might also "refer to the act of **engaging, applying, exercising, realising**, or **practising** ideas."

I take this as my second T in M.A.T.T., to refer to praxis that is Totalising, Transformist and Transitional.

Totalising praxis

All the theories, lessons or skills that we learn will come to nothing if we don't integrate them into our whole way of being in an all-embracing, comprehensive practice. This process of course takes years.

It must happen though.
It must start within each person.
It must become true of the way we operate as groups.
It must also saturate our thinking, our integrated worldview, like I've proposed in THE SPECS.

Theology, **H**istory, **E**conomics, **S**cience, **P**hilosophy, **E**cology, **C**ulture and the **S**ocial Sciences – eventually everything must be seen as a totality, all systems together. That's why insightful collaboration and collective action is essential for sustained progress.

Transformist praxis

First, to be transformist, our praxis must be **oriented to structural change**. Life is organic, pulsating and developing. Our environment (natural and social) is continually changing so over time and at the right time, structures need to change to sustain human flourishing.

Second, our praxis must be informed by critique that is explanatory. This **explanatory critique** seems to happen all the time these days, for example when both sides of a discussion or argument about youth crime, domestic violence, the Voice Referendum, pandemics, military conflicts, climate change, homelessness, etc., try to **explain why** their opponents are wrong or why that social or political problem persists despite so much effort so far.

Critique's much harder than it sounds!

Chapter 8: Making Truth MATTers Entirely Pervade You

Third, our praxis must be informed by a vision of the future that is grounded in the present. The term for that is **concrete utopianism**. With all the problems facing humanity now our vision for a better future must be coherent with what already exists, that is, with what people already know and have. That's the only way we'll be able to persuade each other of the need for change. We must be both optimistic and realistic. But the only way forward is to be relentless as we:

- ✓ combine all THE SPECS
- ✓ be dedicated to communicating and working together with compassion and care such as in my 4 Rs
- ✓ be directed by transformative change and learning along the lines of the 6 principles of Chapter 3

Transitional praxis

At this point in history now more than ever before, it's critical that we hold everything lightly. We can't be married to the way we do things. If our praxis is hindering growth and flourishing, then we must adapt it. That's the meaning of transitional. Our way of being and doing is temporary since we are always open to moving on, open to change from one state or condition to another.

At points in this chapter, I've related stories of where I've pursued truth in relation to micro, macro and meta levels in health for example, across a whole range of actions, and inactions

> These stories and similar ones, all help form
> the backdrop for more workshops
> I look forward to doing with your group in the future

My years' association with specific Asian communities over the past 45 years were highly significant. Writing Chapters 7 and 8 has helped confirm that. Life with friends in those communities taught me so much more about when to act, to pause, to slow down and when to just stop and take rest, regularly. I relished being immersed in very diverse contexts like *Aashiana, Sahara House,* friends from North-east Indian States, and *Satya Niketan School* in Nagod. We didn't always use the exact words, but our common commitment was:

> - Strive for a life of *continual transformation.*
> - With all your hearts and minds, hold fast to a *transformative stance* towards all around you.
> - *Remain trustworthy* in all relationships, teamwork and tasks.

I complete this chapter with mentioning another service agency I've engaged with since 1984, providing many opportunities to observe their praxis.

Malaysian CARE is a non-profit Christian NGO established in 1979. Their Vision, Mission and Ethos are **totalising** and **transformist**, committed to serving the poor and needy irrespective of religion and ethnicity. Observing their workers in action and partnering with them whenever possible, I'm struck with their **transitional** approach in responding with prayer, great care, passion and willingness to take on suffering.

> - Malaysian CARE's focus is on **empowering communities**
> - They aim for **long-term sustainable development**
> - They **see themselves as partners** to the local church and the people they are serving

Chapter 8: Making Truth MATTers Entirely Pervade You

Chapter Summary

- ✓ getting to the truth of a matter can inspire hope of change for a better future
- ✓ to sustain change or transformation, truth must be acted on, hope must deliver
- ✓ your choices and mine must eventually include 7 key components
- ✓ the four components in this chapter deal with an all-pervading vision of transformation
- ✓ they're a foundation for our deepening spiral of consolidating trust and integrity
- ✓ change ultimately begins at the micro level: spirit, mind, cellular, brain, other body systems
- ✓ long-term, choose your own journey integrating natural and other means of self-care
- ✓ transformation is a profound change, hard work and always involves others.

I've outlined in chapters 7 and 8 several agencies and very diverse communities I've known since the late 1970s. Their tremendous passion to sustain collective integrity inspires me. They continue to persevere through both success and failure with a practical vision of transformation that pervades every aspect of their lives.

What might be the best way to sustain such transformation?

Chapter 9 will weave a chain, a web that mutually supports and sustains that vision and its outworking.

For further reading check the relevant links for **Chapter 8** in the **Recommended Reading List**.

Suggestions for Action now

Take some time to write a response to each of the following:

1. Perhaps you've been prompted to reflect on your own journey as you've read of communities in India or Malaysia.
For each one of the **micro, macro or meta** levels, write down what areas you need to act on.

2. On a scale of 1-10, write down where you would assess yourself to be, in relation to these levels of your life situation.

    Discuss your responses with people in your trusted circle of family, friends, or colleagues.

3. Take time to reflect on at least one group you meet with regularly. This can be family members, close friends, social group, or work team for example.

    Now, on a scale of 1-10, meet with them and write down where you would assess yourselves to be as a group, with each of:

    ➢ the three characteristics of **radical agents**, and
    ➢ the three characteristics of **radical praxis**

    Plan within your group, what you might do to take some next steps.

CHAPTER 9

Let Truth MattERS Guide You Through Esteem to Holistic Wellbeing

"Unfortunately, the ideal and expectation that everybody is capable of critical independent thinking, data analysis and having a moral compass, is an assumption that I can't hold anymore in the face of evidence."

Glenn Pearson

CHAPTER 9
Let Truth MattERS Guide You
Through Esteem to Holistic Wellbeing

The truths we trust have vast implications for our sense of worth, our identities and our work in current global contexts. We long for sustainable change. Helping us are paths we **can** take *with the support of others*. It's a matter of continuing to pursue truth.

In Chapter 8 I outlined a practical vision of transformation towards collective integrity pervading every aspect of our lives.

Chapter 9 explores pathways for sustaining such transformations persevering through both success and failure.

Are you passionately committed to extending and sustaining yourselves, your hopes and your goals? Then strive to think and work at deeper levels!

This chapter's main principle is that:

> Our commitment to deeply thinking and living truth
> can strengthen and be strengthened by
> a "multi-directional" sequence or web of qualities or processes
> leading from self-esteem to total well-being.

First, 'depth' is your key to resolving Chapter 8's challenge to sustain transformation.

Chapter 9: Let Truth MattERS Guide You Through Esteem to Holistic Wellbeing

Second, 7 'E's arise from that depth in a chain or web of seven qualities.

Third, being Reflexive (the 'R' in mattERS) or living *dadirri* is your way of living out this web of deep thinking and deep work.

Fourth, 'S' is for each Self being strengthened among yourselves.

Sustain and extend yourselves through deep thinking and deep working

More people were deep thinkers before the age of electronic media!

Deep thinkers tend to:

1. treasure curiosity, asking big, profound, and complex questions
2. love learning, growing, understanding the world and their place in it
3. examine thoughts and feelings, analyse experiences, reflect on actions
4. connect deeply at emotional levels
5. crave meaningful, challenging, yet personal conversations, but love solitude whether alone or in a crowd
6. notice subtle nuances and undercurrents in situations
7. carefully consider and critically analyse all perspectives before forming opinions
8. be comfortable with uncertainty and ambiguity
9. need to beware of overthinking!

Deep workers

Deep work is the ability to focus without distraction on any task requiring deep thinking. How might we develop this habit?

Move beyond good intentions! Yet there are limits to willpower. So, work out what daily routines and rituals will help move you into a state of unbroken concentration ... and maintain it.

Build from the deep – your web of 7 'E's from Esteem to Eudaimonia

Build your life together as a web of 7 'E's.

> The heart
> of your family or other group
> must be grounded in self-esteem and mutual-esteem.
> The strands or links across your web will form your moral compass –
> true, right, just, trustworthy and loving relationships

Think of nodes across your web as: Esteem (self-/mutual-) →Existential security→ Ergonic efficiency →Empowerment →Emancipation→Eudaimonia. I define these below.

The point is not that anyone of us, and certainly not a particular group in history has ever fully lived out these qualities, processes or states of being. **Rather**, they are **qualities of life** we hunger for and the **processes of getting there**. They're what we strive for every day. Yet we rest in knowing that whatever does become reality for us and through us is **a gift from outside of ourselves**.

That said, you might well think of people or whole communities whose way of life tends to shine brighter than others'. Which people or groups might you think of as you read this chapter?

Chapter 9: Let Truth MattERS Guide You Through Esteem to Holistic Wellbeing

E – Introducing the 7 'E's

1. Self-Esteem

This is **not the same as self-love**.

On the one hand, when we're "**in love with ourselves**", others see us as driven by self-interest and overly concerned about others' opinions. Basically:

> *(Self-love) is in love with being loved, detests being disliked, and hungers for power and status. Conceited and intrinsically egoistic, lacking in truthfulness and sincerity, it is premised on the ideological illusion that human subjects are atomistic and opposed (to one another), disconnected from social and natural being.*
> **Mervyn Hartwig**

When we fall into that trap, deep down we suspect we are a fraud. We can become filled with self-loathing for being like that. Yet we long to have a healthy view of ourselves because we know we're made for connection and inter-dependence.

On the other hand, based mainly on the writings of Roy Bhaskar, Mervyn Hartwig **defines self-esteem** in the *Dictionary of Critical Realism* as:

- **grounded in** relations of care, solidarity and trust, and **sustained by** these relations
- an **inner resource** essential for altruism (an unselfish concern for others' welfare)
- **pursuing consistency** between theory and practice
- placing a high priority on **truth** and **freedom** in flourishing

2. Mutual-Esteem

It's clear that your own self-esteem as defined here increases when others respect, affirm and encourage you. Then you're more likely to strengthen others in return by respecting, affirming and encouraging them. We tend to truly appreciate those who hold us in high esteem.

On the downside, when we're impacted by oppressive relationships, we're more likely to oppress others in turn. As it's said, hurt people hurt people.

3. Existential security

Existential security is a **relatively new framework** going beyond ideas of just **human** or **national** security. According to contemporary **global media** it's the very actions of humanity that are threatening the survival or **existence of humanity** as a whole!

Summarising current risks and realities:

- ➢ dangers or threats are **due to human actions**
- ➢ modes of protection must be **mutual restraint** and **resilience**
- ➢ the trusted actors for security are **nation states** and **global political institutions**, and
- ➢ the timeframe is **intergenerational**

In other words, **the challenge** is that all of **humanity**, every **generation**, and all our **institutions** must do everything possible holding each other in high esteem, acting with restraint for a secure future.

4. Ergonic efficiency

Ergonic has to do with the word "work". So, this existential security challenge (the third 'E') can only be met locally and globally (so we're told) as we carefully find ways to **work effectively** and **efficiently** with

Chapter 9: Let Truth MattERS Guide You Through Esteem to Holistic Wellbeing

all our material resources, our people, our energy, our time, our money, on goals that we agree to.

It's as simple and as difficult as that!

5. Empowerment

To be empowered is not the same as being enabled. Enabling simply removes something that constrains or restricts actions. Extra support might also be provided.

Will we only enable or truly empower each other?

Enabling	Empowering
Removes restrictions or supports others not able to do it on their own.	Provides tools and resources for self-sufficiency.
Might perpetuate negative behaviours or habits.	More likely to encourage decision-making and agency.
Might create reliance or dependence on others.	More likely to create autonomy and independence.

6. Emancipation

Think of emancipatory activity as three things.

First, you **think very carefully** about a **radically wholesome society**. You imagine and theorise it along with what systems or structures are hindering changes in that direction

Second, your **hard work** tends to bring about those changes in society. Such work by transformed, transformative and trustworthy people (remember my 6 'T's from chapter 8?) includes researching and most definitely praying (when you believe in praying).

Third, you must **continually cross-fertilise** those first two activities, the thinking and the doing, the theory and the practice.

What is meant by a radically wholesome society? The seventh 'E', for eudaimonia, points in that direction. It also sounds remarkably like emancipatory activity as I've just described it.

7. Eudaimonia

This Greek word literally means "good spirit".

For Aristotle it apparently meant **political action** as well as **intellectual activity**. He claimed we're in a state of eudaimonia not only when we contemplate wisdom and understanding, but also and especially when we apply that wisdom practically and morally for justice, with self-restraint. In other words, Aristotle was describing conditions for **human flourishing** or **well-being**, a term now well known.

Some readers will have words like this in another language. Arnhem Land's Yolŋu have the word *Mägaya*. I highly recommend you look up the site for *Why Warriors* listed in Chapter 6's Recommended Readings.

While writing this chapter I got news of the passing of Dr Dj Gondarra who requested Richard Trudgen to write the book *Why Warriors Lie Down and Die*. Dr Gondarra devoted his life to leading his communities in practicing and explaining the Yolŋu system of Law (*Madayin*) and its relationship to *Mägaya*. This *Madayin*:

- ➢ is seen as holy
- ➢ demands great respect, covering a whole system of law and living
- ➢ encompasses virtually every aspect that Western Law struggles to adapt to
- ➢ was given at creation to establish and maintain a state of *Mägaya*

Chapter 9: Let Truth MattERS Guide You Through Esteem to Holistic Wellbeing

Mägaya is a tranquil state like the surface of a lake without a ripple, wave, or swell, where everyone can live free from threats or hostility. Indigenous languages globally have their own terms for both law and the state of wellbeing it's designed to maintain.

From the Middle East, the Hebrew Shalam or Shalom and the Arabic Salaam similarly imply wellbeing, making things centred and whole and restoring integrity.

So now, along your chain of wellbeing, within your web of 7 'E's, underpin them all with practising **reflexivity**.

R – Be Reflexive throughout your web:
balance your social relationships with social concerns

Every one of us is reflexive every day, at least to some extent. We all have this capacity to:

1. self-consciously monitor our activities
2. deliberate internally as we talk it through within ourselves and
3. reflect deeply on our entire spiritual, natural, practical and social contexts

Australians recently came to hear one very clear way of putting it – *dadirri*.

Many Indigenous languages have a word that means something like 'deep listening'. *Dadirri* is that word in *Ngan'gikurunggurr*, an Australian Northern Territory language.

Dr Miriam Rose Ungunmerr-Baumann advocates this kind of listening – a quiet awareness – summing up a whole way of being. She's a groundbreaking leader in remote Indigenous education, a celebrated painter, activist, and speaker. In 1988 she established the 'Miriam Rose Foundation' to help young Indigenous people 'walk in two worlds'.

As a renowned Aboriginal elder Dr Ungunmerr-Baumann was recognised as the 2021 Senior Australian of the Year, calling on everyone to really *listen* to Indigenous people and pay proper attention to the land we live in.

Whatever approach we take to deep thinking, deep listening, and deep work within our groups, we're invited to:

- recognise that everyone is at least uncertain, confused or even traumatised to some degree
- be ethical, provide a safe space, a safe process and confidentiality for everyone
- understand and respond appropriately in cultural contexts where relationships are reciprocal
- understand the implications of hierarchical structures and respond appropriately
- understand the potential for misusing power either intentionally or unintentionally

I relate one of a few times when I was privileged to participate in such deep work. This book's cover picture (lower) is from that day. The University of Malaysia's Centre for Poverty and Development Studies had asked me to work with Orang Asli communities. In one relatively remote place we sat on the bamboo slat raised flooring of one home for six continuous hours along with village community facilitators.

There were maybe 120 men, women, and children of all ages crammed into the space or looking in through the open window areas as I presented a two-page talk via translation. In essence I'd covered points something like this book. That day in the jungle far from modern society's comforts

Chapter 9: Let Truth MattERS Guide You Through Esteem to Holistic Wellbeing

and props became the clearest demonstration of how a whole group's lifestyle illustrated this book's message:

> ➢ My TRAUMA acronym (Chapter 3)
> ➢ My 4 'R's and 6 principles (Chapter 3)
> ➢ The 6 'T's and 7 'E's (Chapters 8 and 9)

What I adapted and presented was just a catalyst. They expanded on it with strenuous discussion and debate. Their social, economic and political plight was desperate. How might they apply these insights to their lives and take further action?

I've not been able to follow the progress of that relatively remote community. As so often happens in community work however, it was they who taught me afresh about resilience, determination, and the importance of each self in ourselves.

S – Strengthen every Self among yourselves

Look again at the original statement from Chapter 8. We now come to the final letter in truth MATTERS – the 'S' for Selfs or Selves at the heart of everything.

If we're going to sustain transforming trauma together, then Truth MATTERS:

> ➢ through all the micro, macro and meta **levels** of everyone's **Self** (that's yours and mine!)
> ➢ across each **Self's** habitual **actions** and **inactions**
> ➢ building on every **Self's** life as a **radical agent**
> ➢ within each **Self's radical praxis** that mutually strengthens
> ➢ a sequence, chain, or web building from **Self-esteem to total well-being**
> ➢ sustained ultimately by being **reflexive** as **Selves**, personally and together

What does the "self" mean? Who really am I? Who are you?

Some **philosophers** say that the self is an immortal soul while others say it's nothing more than a bundle of perceptions.

Some **psychologists** say there are more than 80 different molecular, neural, psychological and social phenomena about the self that can be explained.

In simple terms we could say that:

- What is called your **ego** is **real**. Yet it's a **partial, potentially false self**, an illusion.
- Your ego resides within your **embodied self**, which is **relatively real**.
- Your **absolute real self** is the totality of who you are **in relationship** actually and potentially with everyone and everything in your environment.

> **This book's purpose**
> is to grapple with what it might mean for each of us as an absolute real self
> to **transform hurt** and **trauma together** with others.
> It will mean being reflexive alone and as groups along this journey.

That's not easy! It includes "deliberating internally" or talking within yourself. One Professor of Sociology, the late Margaret (Maggie) Archer, has written a whole book on this, called "Structure, Agency and the Internal Conversation". She describes **possible conversations** you have **within yourself** as you relate to family, friends, colleagues, then the systems we live and work in every day, like education, health, or in our careers. These are **ways of being reflexive**.

Chapter 9: Let Truth MattERS Guide You Through Esteem to Holistic Wellbeing

The way we deliberate with ourselves can change as we grow and mature. It most likely fluctuates according to our changing **circumstances**, our changing **contexts**, and our changing **concerns**.

Where might you see yourself amongst the following four options? Maggie Archer says there'll be times when:

1. We might **struggle in our attempts** to self-consciously monitor our activities, deliberate internally and reflect deeply on our entire contexts.

   Our personal capacity to be reflexive becomes **impeded, restricted or suspended**. We're not able to take a 'stance' towards society. Archer says that at such times we remain '**fractured reflexives**'.

2. We might develop an **evasive stance** towards our world, where we communicate primarily with others who are similar and familiar to ourselves, while we evade even offers that would advance us in life.

   As '**communicative reflexives**' our top priority becomes **stability** amongst family, friends and associates. Our goal is **social integration**.

3. We might develop a **strategic stance** towards our world where; to fulfil our aims in our work context (e.g. education or health) we take advantage of what will help us while negotiating around what will hinder us.

   As '**autonomous reflexives**' our top priority becomes **systemic development**, improving the social systems that relate to our field of work. We tend to be willing to invest hours of unpaid time towards that goal, often at the cost of our own social relationships.

4. We might develop a **subversive stance** towards our world, where we continue to pay the price for resisting offers that would help or hinder us but at the same time would compromise our core values.

   As such we are '**meta-reflexives**'. Our top priority becomes a **healthy blending of being both evasive and strategic**: we aim for robust systemic development while strengthening social integration. Archer says meta-reflexives consistently hold to their core values such as goodness, truth, compassion, creativity, public service and private well-being.

Do you know meta-reflexive people who hold tenaciously to high standards and human values? Are you one yourself? If so, you risk becoming embittered, disillusioned, or just capitulating to the world and its systems, rather than undergoing consistent transformation.

> *This is a technological age.*
> *Humanity is being devalued at every turn.*
> *Society needs truth and goodness to be constantly awakened*
> *and re-presented as leaven to renew hope.*
> *For only truth lived and spoken in love*
> *will cast out fear and sustain collective integrity.*
>
> **Neil Hockey**

Chapter 9: Let Truth MattERS Guide You Through Esteem to Holistic Wellbeing

Chapter Summary

- **It's possible** for any group to sustain collective integrity.
- We must **persevere** through both success and apparent failure.
- Deep thinking and deep working are **keys to living** transformative truth.
- That deep well can give rise to **a web of the 7 'E's**.
- We are **all vulnerable** to weaknesses in any part of this web.
- Strengthen this web through **reflexivity**, the capacity we all possess to quietly observe, listen deeply, and contemplate to inform our actions as a way of life.
- In a world of increasing stress and trauma, our reflexive selves desperately need to be gently (if possible) nurtured **beyond being fractured**.
- Being reflexive is risky. The world and its systems tend to keep us **preoccupied with ourselves** by **either** (a) **evading** both perceived threats and potential benefits to our private worlds, **or** (b) **strategically engaging** those world systems at the expense of our social connections.
- Being **meta-reflexive** is the most transformative stance we can take. That's when we subvert the world and its systems by being **both evasive and strategic**; we aim for robust systemic development while also strengthening social integration.

For further reading check the relevant links for **Chapter 9** in the **Recommended Reading List**.

Suggestions for Action now

1. List three areas of your life (home life, work, social, etc) where you are challenged to think and work more deeply.

2. Discuss your responses with people in your trusted circle of family, friends, or colleagues.

3. Read back over and take time to think deeply about my description of the 7 'E's. On a scale of 1-10, evaluate together your group's commitment to work further (as a priority) on each of the following areas:

    1) Self Esteem
    2) Mutual Esteem
    3) Existential security
    4) Ergonic efficiency
    5) Empowerment
    6) Emancipation
    7) Eudaimonia

4. Choose just one (or more) of those areas above.

    What actions will you commit to working on personally for the next one month?

    Now share these actions with each other.

5. Write down your commitments from the previous step, including:

    - ✓ how you will hold each other accountable, and
    - ✓ when you will do so

CHAPTER 10

Now What?

"At the core of the crisis facing our nations
is the fact that we are being led away from
our traditional ideals by the people with the
authority to control our lives.
Some of these people ...
are the very people we count on
to provide leadership and embody the values
at the heart of our societies –
to love and sacrifice for their people."

Taiaiake Alfred,
in *Peace, Power, Righteousness*

CHAPTER 10
Now What?

> Hard times are coming,
> when we'll be wanting the voices of writers who
> can see alternatives to how we live now,
> can see through our fear-stricken society and its obsessive technologies
> to other ways of being,
> and even imagine real grounds for hope.
> We'll need writers who can remember freedom – poets, visionaries –
> realists of a larger reality.
>
> **Ursula K. Le Guin**

Farmers know what it means to break up the fallow ground. A field left idle for some time must be ploughed in and cleared of thorns, preparing it for even greater productivity.

Where is your fallow ground?

My life's been a series of lessons in discerning some roots of taboo trauma, dealing with them to regenerate and sustain integrity with others.

Here's my summary invitation and final call to action from this workbook.

Chapter 1 revealed my personal journey in negotiating taboo trauma with its roots in domestic, political, and colonial violence. Today there are calls for truth-telling everywhere.

Chapter 10: Now What?

Get together with others and commit to investigating the things that concern you most, using THE SPECS by blending

Theology
History
Economics

Science
Philosophy
Ecology
Culture and
Social Science

to help discern and guide this challenging pathway to growth.

Chapter 2 posed the need to question people.

- ✓ Probe their persuasive arguments
- ✓ Weed out widespread propaganda
- ✓ Search for trustworthy sources of truth

Ask open-ended or strategic questions to build this trust, opening insights into the truth of multigenerational legacies of trauma.

Chapter 3 recounted my pursuit of truth through radical-conservative faith relationships. Over many years I learned ways of disarming trauma's triggers. I highly recommend to you this protective layer of T.R.A.U.M.A.

- ➤ **T**arget your limbic system
- ➤ **R**eclaim generational strengths
- ➤ **A**ctivate positive values
- ➤ **U**nderstand behaviour patterns
- ➤ **M**aximise positive potentials and
- ➤ **A**chieve what you can for the moment

In your family, workplace or other team whether long-established or just forming, hold the four 'R' assumptions uppermost:

1. **Realise** what trauma is and how it can affect people and groups
2. **Recognise** the signs of trauma
3. **Respond** to trauma by having an appropriate system of strategies, and
4. **Resist** re-traumatising anyone

As you work with your group to support recovery from trauma, apply the six principles consistently:

1. **Safety** and **Security**
2. **Trustworthiness** and **Transparency**
3. **Peer Support**
4. **Collaboration** and **Mutuality**
5. **Empowerment, Voice,** and **Choice**
6. **Cultural** and **Historical issues**

Remember to discuss what your organisation might do to habitually improve their outcomes.

Chapter 4 helps you get clear on journeys of working together. Since trust is at times betrayed, take three steps to gain a clearer, broader view of what it takes to ride out such storms.

1. Get clear on your **definitions** of integrity, trust, and aspects of love.
2. Indigenous history can teach us a lot. Truly see and embrace their **perspectives on the need for hope** as a basis for integrity, trust, and love.
3. In your group there will be some people whose history includes stories of great suffering. Ask each other what you are learning

Chapter 10: Now What?

from Indigenous or other perspectives on **the role of truth** as a basis for hope within suffering.

Chapter 5 prompts your group to ask how **you** might explain truth in practice in a 'post-truth' world, if you are to live with common hope and purpose.

I used the British PM's 2023 coronation speech to provoke thinking about whatever issues are a priority for your group. Understanding **ideas** about a problem are important, but ultimately you must grapple with **observable, practical realities** by **asking questions**:

1. What first-hand data do you have, especially people's lived experiences?
2. How can this data be explained?
3. What are some reasons or causes for what's been observed, even over decades or centuries?

Remember that identifying and critiquing causes can raise your hopes for change.

My next acronym reinforced this through **5 key aspects of living out truth,** which **form a deepening spiral of hope.**

> Truth as
> Reality
> Unlocks, Uncarths, and Uncovers
> Trembling, Tentative, and Total
> Hearts and Hopes

My challenge to you now is, what will it take to get to the truth, the basic structures at work within and behind **whatever issues cause you greatest concern**?

Chapter 6 provides an example of how identity and integrity might be regenerated through struggling with truth in everyday realities where truth is denied. The chapter returns to discourse around the 2023 king's coronation in historical colonial contexts. These contexts have **implications way beyond Indigenous experiences**.

What might you do now as a family, group or team, with your deeper insights into:

- the meaning of lawful as opposed to legal
- grieving as a hard road engaging truth, restoring identity and regenerating integrity?

Chapter 7 introduces you to a little of my journey in restoring and consolidating trust, pursuing truth to sustain integrity as communities living through traumatic times. The context is Asia, but the lessons are applicable anywhere and everywhere.

Your call is to adapt and adopt these lessons as daily habits.

Chapter 8 puts to you the question:

> How might you best sustain
> entirely pervading transformation towards collective integrity
> (your hope in action)
> through life's inevitable rhythms
> of success and failure?

This pervading transformation involves:

- living life to the full at **Micro, Macro** and **Meta** levels
- developing habitual **Actions** and **in-Actions**

Chapter 10: Now What?

- ✓ as **Transformed, Transformative** and **Trustworthy** people grounded through
- ✓ **Totalising, Transformist,** and **Transitional** praxis

Chapter 9 supports a pathway to fulfilling that challenge:

- ➢ Sustain and extend yourselves through **deep thinking** and **deep working**
- ➢ Build together a chain or web of **7 'E's from Esteem to Eudaimonia**
- ➢ Consciously practice **meta-reflexivity** as a way of sustaining both your social connections and your wider social awareness and concerns for justice

Your next step?

Apply this book with others at your own pace. Focus on what you need to for the moment. It's potentially a lifetime of work. Make uncertainty, stress or trauma be another gateway to discerning what is right, just, safe, good, trustworthy and true.

Your world needs more leaders, righteous and courageous. Join them!

I'd be delighted to continue conversations with you about any topic or thread of interest from this book.

Email me hello@transformingtraumatogether.com

Or via www.neilhockey.com

Live Passionately
Think Deeply
for Lasting Change!

RECOMMENDED READING LIST

Following is a small sample of relevant readings for each chapter. I focus on those that have been mentioned in the book. Use these or similar ones as springboards for further reading and action.

Introduction

Hockey, Neil (2023) Sustaining Spirit across Complexities of International Development in Relation to Indigenous Peoples. (An academic read, with plain version to come!)

Chapter 1 – Intuiting Trauma's Journey into Truth

https://integratedlistening.com/what-is-trauma/

https://www.youtube.com/watch?v=BJfmfkDQb14

https://letsreimagine.org/blog/taboos-hard-things

https://www.psychologytoday.com/us/blog/the-flourishing-family/202107/breaking-the-chains-generational-trauma

https://blueknot.org.au › newsletters › silenced-not-silent

https://www.abc.net.au/listen/programs/news-specials/-not-silent-but-silenced-first-nations-front-line-services-want-/104231504

Van der Kolk, Bessel (2014) The Body Keeps the Score.

https://en.wikipedia.org/wiki/2021_Australian_Parliament_House_sexual_misconduct_allegations

https://aihw.gov.au/family-domestic-and-sexual-violence

https://andnowwhat.be/about/glossary/ - "Trauma"; "Wicked Challenges"; "Wicked Problems"

https://waterscenterst.org Waters Center for Systems Thinking

https://www.weforum.org/agenda/2023/07/systems-thinking-education-future/?+Skills+and+Learning

https://www.weforum.org/agenda/2021/01/what-systems-thinking-actually-means-and-why-it-matters-today/

Chapter 2 – People, Persuasion or Propaganda: Whose Truth Might we Trust?

Atkinson, Judy (2002) Trauma Trails, Recreating Songlines.

Coaldrake, Peter (2022) https://www.coaldrakereview.qld.gov.au. Report into the Qld Public Sector

Ellul, Jacques (1973) Hope in Time of Abandonment.

Gish, Art (1970) The New Left and Christian Radicalism.

Hockey, Neil (2007) Learning for Liberation.

Sharp, Gene (1973) The Politics of Nonviolent Action.

Sharp, Gene (1980) Social Power and Political Freedom.

Trudgen, Richard (2000) Why Warriors Lie Down and Die.

Tully, Tracy (2020). FEARless: Buckle Up … Build Resilience.

Chapter 3 – Collectively Cultivate Hope's Roots (for Trust and Love)

Dann, Robert (2004) Father of Faith Missions.

Leaf, Caroline (2013) Switch on Your Brain.

https://www.britannica.com/science/limbic-system

Recommended Reading List

https://www.nicabm.com

https://retrainingthebrain.com

https://www.verywellmind.com/what-is-a-genogram-5217739

https://www.terryberry.com/blog/how-put-core-values-practice-10-effective-strategies/

https://www.entrepreneur.com/leadership/how-to-activate-and-align-your-values-when-under-pressure/438139

https://www.nchv.org/images/uploads/Research_Brief_61_-_SAMHSA_Trauma_Care.pdf

https://onlinenursing.duq.edu/blog/what-are-the-6-principles-of-trauma-informed-care/

Department of Families Fairness and Housing Victoria | Framework for trauma-informed practice (dffh.vic.gov.au)

What is trauma-informed care? - Principles for effective support (nsw.gov.au)

https://www.health.nsw.gov.au/mentalhealth/psychosocial/principles/Pages/trauma-informed.aspx

https://www.blueknot.org.au/Workers-Practitioners/For-Health-Professionals/Resources-for-Health-Professionals/Trauma-Informed-Care-and-practice

Chapter 4 – Getting Clear on the Journey: Trust Betrayed?

Alfred, Taiaiake (1999) Peace, Power, Righteousness.

Hockey, Neil (1998) https://catalogue.nla.gov.au/catalog/1925722 Report on the Trial Syllabus Evaluation.

www.neilhockey.com

https://www.dictionary.com/e/greek-words-for-love/

Otto, Rudolf (1923) The Idea of the Holy.

West, Japanangka Errol (2000) An Alternative to Existing Australian Research and Teaching Models.

Chapter 5 – Matters of T.R.U.T.H.

https://www.sarahjacksoncoaching.com

Bhaskar, Roy (1993/2008) Dialectic: The Pulse of Freedom.

Hartwig, Mervyn (ed.) (2007) Dictionary of Critical Realism.

Mayo, Thomas and O'Brien, Kerry (2023) The Voice to Parliament Handbook.

Miller, Barbara (2023) Voice, Treaty, Truth: Has the Christian Voice Been Heard?

Russell, Bertrand @ https://wisdomquotes.net/philosophy-quotes/

https://www.telegraph.co.uk/royal-family/2023/05/06/rishi-sunak-king-coronation-proud-expression-of-history/

https://www.royal.uk/sites/default/files/documents/2023-05/23-24132%20Coronation%20Liturgy_05%20May_0.pdf

https://www.bible.com The Bible

https://www.britannica.com/topic/postmodernism-philosophy

Recommended Reading List

Chapter 6 – Identity and Integrity Through Truth

https://grammarhow.com/lawful-vs-legal/

https://www.facebook.com/WhyWarriors

https://www.whywarriors.com.au/.../Yolngu_Law_38_Statutes...

https://www.whywarriors.com.au/learn/cultural-awareness-skills/100qa/

https://www.abc.net.au/news/2023-05-19/stan-grant-media-target-racist-abuse-coronation-coverage-enough/102368652?fbclid=IwAR0KJbzZGS7RUsyXTED-6_7uF5GToFM1dSdQ-eCAnsScAjSDPyR5cmbm4pY

https://www.abc.net.au/religion/glimpses-of-something-beyond-strange-faith-of-nick-cave/102252814

Chapter 7 – Restoring Trust, Pursuing Truth

Andrews, Dave (1996/2017) Building A Better World.

Andrews, Dave (2006) Compassionate Community Work: an introductory course for Christians.

Andrews, Dave (2007) Living Community: an introductory course in community work.

Andrews, Dave (2021) To Right Every Wrong.

https://www.goodreads.com/quotes/219323-hope-is-not-a-lottery-ticket-you-can-sit-on

https://www.aljazeera.com/news/2023/7/20/outrage-in-india-over-video-of-manipur-women-paraded-naked-raped

https://www.aljazeera.com/opinions/2023/7/22/can-manipur-ever-trust-india-again

https://www.hindustantimes.com/india-news/protests-escalate-in-india-over-gruesome-rape-of-doctor-101723702950893.html

https://www.satyaniketan.edu.in/about/

Chapter 8 – Truth MATTers: Entirely Pervading Transformations

https://www.independent.co.uk/news/people/roy-bhaskar-philosopher-whose-school-of-critical-realism-challenged-established-ways-of-thinking-about-being-and-knowledge-10009456.html

https://www.verywellhealth.com/mitochondria-function-8409605

https://www.aima.net.au

https://academic.oup.com/jac/article/67/9/2062/880174?login=false

https://www.malaysiancare.org

Chapter 9 – Truth MattERS: From Self/Mutual Esteem to Wholistic Wellbeing

Archer, Margaret (2003) Structure, Agency and the Internal Conversation.

Hari, Johann (2022) Stolen Focus: Why You Can't Pay Attention.

https://ideapod.com/signs-youre-a-deep-thinker-according-to-psychology/

https://calnewport.com/deep-work-rules-for-focused-success-in-a-distracted-world/

https://calnewport.com/my-new-book-digital-minimalism/

Hartwig, Mervyn (2007) Dictionary of Critical Realism - on "self-esteem", then "subjectivity".

https://annemckeown.com/empowering-vs-enabling/

https://www.miriamrosefoundation.org.au/about-miriam-rose-foundation/

Chapter 10 – Now What?

Le Guin, Ursula K (2019) https://www.ursulakleguin.com/words-are-my-matter

RESOURCES

Listed are some resources you can use in being a transformative influence in the world.

First are my FREE bonus offers.

Second, I give some history of *Transform the Nations* in Asia. Check out their website. You too can get involved there or elsewhere.

Third, SmashGo is the company that first put me in touch with Andrew Carter and the Global Publishing Group. Both teams provide great support for anyone in business.

There is no shortcut to growth. You won't encourage a plant or tree to produce faster by pulling it up to check its root system every week. Give it appropriate nutrients and conditions however and see what happens.

Engage with others, draw on their resources and skills to consolidate your journey in transformation. I personally recommend each of these samples below.

FREE Bonus Offers
Worth over $550 for YOU

This workbook can't contain all that needs to be said, or what I want to say, or what is relevant to you at this time. I encourage you to continue with action at every stage, in every chapter.

So, I've included these wonderful FREE offers for you. Don't miss out: act TODAY.

By going to my website or using the QR code below, or emailing me, you will get access to:

- ✓ Up to 30-minutes online or by phone with me, completely obligation free, regarding the issues you or your group are working through right now. Given modern technology, this can be from anywhere in the world.

- ✓ A digital download of an incredible bonus chapter that includes (a) stories of how some of the book's questions or challenges are working out in my situations, and (b) what it can mean to walk with one another through transforming trauma one-to-one, or in families, teams and organisations over many years if necessary. This chapter is not available anywhere else.

- ✓ Three months of weekly e-classes based on this book.

I'd be delighted to continue conversations with you about any topic or thread of interest from this book.

Contact me via hello@transformingtraumatogether.com
my website www.neilhockey.com
or just scan this QR code

Live Passionately
Think Deeply
for Lasting Change!

A brief history of Transform the Nations

2009 - *Educate Nepal* set up as an Australian ministry, to train teachers and develop faith-based schools in Asia.

2011 - *Transform the Nations Ltd.* (TtN), established to protect, educate and train exploited, impoverished and vulnerable children.

2012 - in partnerships, TtN set up a rescue work, a halfway house with vocational training for trafficked, and at-risk, impoverished women.

November 2012 - TtN invited to assist in developing private schools in **Myanmar,** training teachers to establish a system of private schools and training centres.

August 2016 - 'Promise' (now at https://covenantyangon.com), an international school was established and gained Cambridge accreditation early in 2017.

2023 – TtN's schools in Myanmar transitioned to become Covenant Schools.

Nepal
The trafficking of children has become a way of life for many marginalised families who are trying to survive, exploited and forced into a living nightmare.... with no voice or hope. Partnering with different organisations, TtN gives them that voice and hope, offering a way out of human slavery, opening opportunities for quality education, vocational training and a safe new environment in which to heal, grow and transform.

Myanmar
Rescuing abused girls, young ladies and helping widows has created opportunities for employment and self-sustainability, with education a key. Schools are set up to give learning opportunities to the needy, the orphaned and the wider community through sponsorship where needed.

Thailand
A school dedicated to meeting the educational needs of displaced Burmese students opened in Mae Sot in August 2022. Current facilities are already outgrown, so leadership are raising funds to erect a purpose-built facility to serve the refugee school and university students in their care.

Note: All TtN **Australian administrative staff are volunteers.** 50% of this book's proceeds will be donated to TtN.

To donate to this work, go to https://www.transformthenations.org/ways-to-give

Business Owners Smashing It Online

Webinar Series

This webinar series hosted by Nik Cree, founder of SmashGo.co offers FREE weekly sessions designed to help business owners and entrepreneurs learn and master the digital tools and strategies needed to grow and scale their businesses.

Each session attracts 25 to 55+ RSVPs, with additional viewers tuning in on Facebook Livestreams and YouTube replays.

What to Expect
Valuable takeaways for all participants, with guest experts sharing insights and strategies you can apply immediately. You'll also explore new apps and tools in the "Cool Online Tools" segment—designed to help you save time, cut costs, and streamline operations.

What You'll Learn

Practical knowledge on:
- Using online tools to simplify operations
- Effective marketing strategies for business growth
- Building networks for referrals and leads
- Step-by-step advice on leveraging digital tools efficiently

How to Join or Watch

RSVP to a live event on Zoom:
https://ezyurl.co/bosio

Watch replays on YouTube:
https://www.youtube.com/@smashgo

Don't miss out—register today.

ABOUT THE AUTHOR
Author, Speaker, Facilitator, Mentor, Teacher

Neil is passionate about community development, engagement and education. He has done extensive community work in India, Malaysia, and Australia, as well as high school teaching in Australia and India over the course of his working life.

The dux of his high school, Neil went on to obtain degrees in Science, Arts and Education, as well as a PhD in a Transformative Philosophy of Truth. He co-founded the Sahara House Centre for Residential Care and Rehabilitation in New Delhi in 1978, remaining there for six years. This experience strengthened his passion for community work and over the next 40 years he has worked with multiple government and non-government organisations to help trauma-impacted people and their families in India, Malaysia and Australia.

In addition, he was a visiting Research Fellow at the University of Malaysia's Centre for Poverty and Development Studies for two years, as well as the Copy Editor for the University's Journal of Institutions and Economies.

Neil also played a key role in helping establish multiple Indigenous community-controlled programs in the Logan-Beaudesert region of South-East Queensland and was a State-wide evaluator of the Trial Senior Syllabus in Aboriginal and Torres Strait Islander Studies in the mid-1990s. As he did internationally, Neil has regularly worked alongside numerous private and public sector agencies in his home country to improve health, education, youth and community justice, and employment and training outcomes with Indigenous Australians.

He has presented on community development, engagement, and education at 14 international conferences in 10 different countries over the past two decades. Neil is a member of the IACR (International Association of Critical Realism) and the TPAQ (Teachers' Professional Association of Queensland).

Marrying into a Chinese Malaysian family more than 40 years ago, Neil has two children and three grandchildren. He has lived, worked and travelled extensively throughout India and Malaysia.

www.ingramcontent.com/pod-product-compliance
Ingram Content Group UK Ltd.
Pitfield, Milton Keynes, MK11 3LW, UK
UKHW020010160325
456262UK00006B/474